# Discovering the Franciscan Intellectual Tradition: A Life-Giving Vision

John V. Kruse

Published in the United States
by Franciscan Institute Publications
St. Bonaventure University, St. Bonaventure, NY 14778

© 2017 Franciscan Institute Publications,
St. Bonaventure University

All rights reserved.
No part of this book may be reproduced or transmitted in any form or by any means, electronic or mechanical, without permission in writing from the publisher.

Cover Image "St. Francis in the Desert Night"
Jane Cassidy, Indigo Gallery
Jane Cassidy's paintings can be viewed online at www.janecassidystudio.com
and at Indigo Gallery, Madrid, New Mexico

Cover design by Jill M. Smith

ISBN: 978-1-57659-416-2
eISBN: 978-1-57659-417-9

Library of Congress Cataloging-in-Publication Data

Names: Kruse, John V., author.
Title: Introducing the Franciscan intellectual tradition : origins,
    essentials, and importance / John V. Kruse.
Description: St. Bonaventure : Franicscan Institute Publications, 2017.
Identifiers: LCCN 2017015509 | ISBN 9781576594162 (pbk. : alk. paper)
Subjects: LCSH: Franciscans--History. | Franciscans--Intellectual life.
Classification: LCC BX3606.3 .K78 2017 | DDC 271/.3--dc23 LC record available at https://lccn.loc.gov/2017015509

Printed and bound in the United States of America
Franciscan Institute Publications makes every effort
to use environmentally responsible suppliers and materials
in the publishing of its books. This book is printed on acid-free, recycled paper that is
FSC (Forest Stewardship Council) certified.

It is printed with soy-based ink.

# Table of Contents

| | |
|---|---:|
| Acknowledgements | 5 |
| Introduction: <br> Asking Questions of Ultimate Human Concern | 7 |
| Chapter 1 <br> Foundations of a Tradition: The Lives of Francis and Clare | 9 |
| Chapter 2 <br> A Tradition Develops: Main Figures and Key Characteristics | 23 |
| Chapter 3 <br> So What?: Why the Franciscan Intellectual Tradition Matters | 41 |
| Conclusion | 67 |
| Endnotes | 69 |
| Selected Bibliography | 75 |

## Acknowledgements

Gratitude is owed to many who have served as an inspiration for this book and who have helped to make its publication possible. I am eternally grateful to Fr. J. Wayne Hellmann, OFM Conv., for first introducing me to the Franciscan Intellectual Tradition. I extend thanks to the Sisters of Saint Francis of Philadelphia, who sponsor Neumann University and serve as living witnesses to the richness of the Tradition. Thanks also to Fr. John Cella, OFM, Director of Franciscan Pilgrimage Programs, for the opportunity to encounter the sacred sites of Francis and Clare, an encounter which has deeply impacted my understanding of the Franciscan Intellectual Tradition and of its relevance in the modern world. I am very much indebted to Fr. Dominic Monti, OFM, and Br. F. Edward Coughlin, OFM, for their insightful feedback and suggestions as they reviewed early drafts of this work. This project would not have come to fruition without the support of the Commission of the Franciscan Intellectual Tradition (CFIT) and the efforts of both Fr. David Couturier, OFM Cap., and Ms. Jill Smith of Franciscan Institute Publications. Lastly, I extend special gratitude to Sr. Kathleen Moffat, OSF, not only for her editorial insights and design work but most importantly for her guiding inspiration and encouragement during the writing process.

Please note that within this publication, footnotes are identified with Arabic Numerals, while endnotes are identified with Roman Numerals.

# Introduction: Asking Questions of Ultimate Human Concern

Why am I on this planet? How do I lead a meaningful and purposeful life?

These might seem like strange questions to ask at the beginning of a book exploring the Franciscan Intellectual Tradition. In fact, however, these questions are not irrelevant to the Franciscan Intellectual Tradition. You may have asked yourself these or other similar "big questions of life": What happens when we die? Is there a God? If so, how do I find God? What makes something good and something else bad? Why do good people suffer?

Humans have been asking these types of questions since humans have existed. In fact, asking these questions of ultimate concern is part of what makes us human. Throughout time, different people have approached these issues differently and come to their own conclusions. Furthermore, people from all different backgrounds continue to wrestle with these important life issues. Many people today are finding that different contemporary worldviews are not offering satisfactory answers to questions of ultimate meaning. In this book, we will examine how the particular approach called the Franciscan Intellectual Tradition has engaged questions of ultimate human concern. This Franciscan Intellectual Tradition is the framework used by those who have been influenced by the life of St. Francis of Assisi (1181-1226) as they have wrestled with the big questions of life. This book will offer a fuller description of the Franciscan Intellectual Tradition as we proceed.

How could the life of Francis, someone who lived 800 years ago, be relevant to our own lives? In Chapter 1 of this book, we will start out with a brief look at the life of St. Francis and his close friend St. Clare (1194-1253). Within this same chapter, we will identify essential components of the worldview of these two key spiritual figures. In Chapter 2, we will explore how a more systematic way of thinking grew up around the worldview and spirituality[1] of Francis and Clare. In short, this is where the "intellectual" component of the Franciscan Intellectual Tradition

---

[1] Spirituality relates to how one understands and expresses one's spiritual life.

comes in. In Chapter 3, we will discover the relevancy of the Franciscan Intellectual Tradition by exploring the life-giving insights that it provides into questions of ultimate human concern.

We turn now to the lives of Francis and Clare, the inspiration of the Franciscan Intellectual Tradition, whose world bore many similarities to our own and who wrestled with many of the same issues we continue to wrestle with today.

## QUESTIONS FOR REFLECTION AND DISCUSSION:

1. What do you know about the life of St. Francis?
2. What do you consider to be the two most important questions of life?
3. Where do you look for answers to the most important questions of life?

# Chapter 1 – Foundations of a Tradition: The Lives of Francis and Clare

You may have heard of St. Francis, you may have seen a statue of him in a garden, and you may have asked yourself what this saint often associated with animals who lived hundreds of years ago could possibly have to do with your own life. This is an important question to ask. In some senses, the world of Francis and his friend Clare was very different from our own. Clearly, the world has changed considerably in 800 years. Yet, in other ways, the world of Francis and Clare was quite similar to our own. Francis and Clare lived in a time in which society was going through substantial changes. Their world was plagued by wars resulting from class tensions, political struggles, and even religious differences. Furthermore, Francis and Clare lived in a world that expected them to fit into certain categories and to fulfill certain preconceived roles without making too many waves within the way things were.

## The Lives of Francis and Clare

In order to understand the Franciscan Intellectual Tradition (FIT), we have to know about the lives of Francis and Clare, the lives on which the FIT is based. Francis was born in 1181 in Assisi, a small city in central Italy.

Prior to this period, there were basically two social classes: the land-owning nobility (the *majores*) and the working lower class (the *minores*). Around the time of Francis, a new social class was beginning to emerge from within the *minores*: the merchant (or business) class. These commoners began to advance their social position through their involvement in the commerce that was rapidly increasing in Europe at the time. Francis was born into such a merchant family. His father was a cloth merchant of considerable wealth. As a young man, Francis was very popular among his peers and seemed to have been somewhat of what we might call a "partier" today. He definitely enjoyed having a good time with his friends and found his greatest pleasures in the material aspects of life.

However, Francis began to undergo a process of conversion that challenged this rather superficial approach to life. When Francis was a young man, a war developed between Assisi, controlled by its merchant class, and the neighboring city of Perugia, controlled by members of the nobility. As was expected of one his age, Francis eagerly took part in the battle. In the course of the war, Francis was captured and taken prisoner of war. During his time of imprisonment, he became quite ill. Sick, imprisoned, and cut off from contact with the outside world, Francis had much time to think about the world in which he lived and the direction of his life. This time of reflection and the experience of being an ill prisoner of war was clearly significant in his personal conversion.

Upon being freed from prison, Francis still had aspirations of becoming a knight, which was the most revered and heroic pursuit a member of his social class could possibly undertake at that time, as it brought him closer to the nobility. Becoming a knight was not cheap. The armor for such a position was expensive and would have to have been paid for by his father. As Francis went off to join the military forces, he is said to have had a dream in which he heard a voice ask him if he would rather serve the servant or the master (i.e., would he rather serve other humans or would he rather serve God). Francis chose serving the master (God) and asked what he should do. The voice in the dream instructed Francis to return to Assisi to follow God's command. It is said that he gave his expensive military armor to a man who was too poor to afford it and returned to Assisi.[2]

At this time in his life Francis was beginning to withdraw more from his friends and spend more time wandering and thinking in the fields and forests surrounding Assisi. He was not finding as much pleasure and fulfillment in "worldly" things, such as celebrating with his friends, as he once did. He was looking for deeper meaning and purpose in his life. There was one particular event that had special significance in his life and his process of conversion. As has been noted, Francis enjoyed the "good

---

[2] Mark Galli, *Francis of Assisi and His World*, (Downers Grove, IL: InterVarsity Press, 2002), 25.

life" of the merchant class and associating with his social peers. There was one group of people, however, that he found to be particularly repulsive: lepers, those who suffered from the disease commonly known as leprosy. Lepers experienced the rotting of their flesh and perhaps even the eventual loss of body parts. The stench associated with leprosy would have been horrific. Lepers, the lowest of the low among the lower-class *minores*, were ostracized by society and forced to live apart in their own communities; they were required to make noise with bells or wooden clappers to let those without leprosy know that "unclean people" were approaching. In his early life, Francis wanted to have nothing to do with lepers and would go far out of his way to avoid them. At one point, however, he did something startling when he saw a leper. Rather than avoid the leper, Francis descended from his horse to embrace the leper. In his own words, he states, "The Lord gave me, Brother Francis, thus to begin doing penance in this way: for when I was in sin, it seemed too bitter for me to see lepers. And the Lord Himself led me among them and I showed mercy to them. And when I left them, what had seemed bitter to me was turned into sweetness of soul and body."[3] This clearly was a

---

[3] Francis of Assisi, *The Testament*, in *Francis of Assisi: Early Documents – The Saint*, vol. 1, eds. Regis J. Armstrong, J.A. Wayne Hellmann, and William J. Short (New York:

life-changing experience. He found the genuine joy and fulfillment that comes from entering into the suffering of the marginalized and rejected. Francis had found God revealed among the poor and lowly of the world and later often ministered to (or "served") lepers.

As Francis sought to find deeper meaning in his life through an ever-intensifying relationship with God, he often prayed in churches in and around Assisi. Some of these churches were falling into disrepair. Yet another significant event in his overall process of conversion occurred when he was praying in the church of San Damiano just outside of the walls of Assisi.

New City Press, 1999), lines 1-3, 124.

While he was at prayer before a crucifix in the church, he heard Jesus speak, "Francis, don't you see that my house is being destroyed? Go, then, and rebuild it for me."[4] Francis at first took this command literally to mean that he should work at rebuilding the dilapidated church of San Damiano. It was only later in his life that he realized that Jesus was calling him to rebuild or reform God's real dwelling place: the People of God. His repair of the church of San Damiano and other churches in and around Assisi, however, required money for building materials. He obtained this "funding" through selling cloth materials that belonged to his father, Pietro di Bernadone. Eventually, Francis' father could no longer tolerate the behavior of his son who appeared to be growing increasingly irrational and deranged. After bringing Francis before the bishop of Assisi, who was to act as a judge, and before the people of Assisi, Francis' father demanded that his son return all that he had taken from him. In an act of deep symbolic significance, Francis stripped himself naked and handed his clothing over to his father as he said, "Until now I have called you father here on earth, but now I can say without reservation, '*Our Father who art in heaven,*' since I have placed all my treasure and hope in him."[5] Francis had completely turned his back on a world of wealth and privilege in order to devote himself entirely to the service of God.

Francis set out to live a life of absolute poverty. He had no actual home but lived in caves or in the countryside. With no possessions that he could call his own, he lived off of the land, working as a day laborer or begging for food and other basic necessities. He wanted nothing that could interfere with his relationship with God. He was open to going wherever God called him and serving God's people in whatever ways God wished, which at this time mainly involved ministering to the lepers or rebuilding small country chapels. He lived in total recognition of his utter dependence on God. While some people considered Francis a madman because of his radical lifestyle, others were impressed by his complete abandonment to God and, seeking to experience the joy and peace that Francis experienced, began to follow him in his way of life. By 1209 there were twelve of them. Desiring to serve as traveling preachers beyond the immediate area of Assisi, they went to Rome to seek approval of their way of life from the Pope. Francis and his "Lesser Brothers" settled below Assisi, at a chapel near the hospices for lepers called the "little portion" (Portiuncula) that was dedicated to St. Mary of the Angels.

---

[4] *The Legend of the Three Companions*, in *Francis of Assisi: Early Documents – The Founder*, vol. 2, eds. Regis J. Armstrong, J.A. Wayne Hellmann, and William J. Short (New York: New City Press, 2000), chap. V, line 13, 76.

[5] Bonaventure, *The Major Legend of Saint Francis*, FA:ED II, chap. 2, line 4, 538.

At first Francis' followers were men, but in 1212 Clare di Favarone (1194-1253), the daughter of a noble family, decided to embrace his life of complete poverty as well. As a noble woman, Clare was expected to marry a member of another noble family so as to increase the power and prestige of her own family or to become a nun in an established form of religious life. However, after conversations with Francis and much to her family's dismay, on the evening of Palm Sunday, 1212, Clare snuck out of her home in the upper area of Assisi and descended down the slopes of Mount Subasio into the valley below Assisi to the Portiuncula. Here Clare assumed the garment of beggars that was worn by Francis and his brothers. Francis also cut Clare's hair as a sign of her total surrender to God, renunciation of the values of society, and embrace of Francis' life of complete poverty. As a woman living in the medieval period, social conventions absolutely prevented Clare from living with Francis and his brothers. Eventually, Clare settled in the church of San Damiano where Francis had originally heard Jesus' call to go rebuild his house. There she established a monastery for women who chose to follow her in living Franciscan poverty. Clare and her "sisters" owned nothing and did not even have the "luxury" of being able to roam about to beg for food and other needs as Francis and his brothers could. Rather, Clare and her sisters were absolutely dependent on God to provide for them through a small garden that they tended and through the generosity of others, including Francis and his brothers. While Francis and his brothers were actively engaged with the world around them through service to the sick and poor and through preaching, Clare and her sisters expressed a more contemplative[6] dimension of Franciscan spirituality through lives dedicated to prayer and service to each other while also responding to the needs of the community outside of the monastery of San Damiano to the degree that they were able.

As part of his active engagement with the world, Francis set out to join the Fifth Crusade in Egypt in 1219. The crusades were a long series of wars spearheaded by Christians to retake the Holy Land (the land of the Bible and of Jesus) from Muslims who had occupied it in the 7th century. Francis witnessed the atrocities of war in Egypt and was shocked by the brutality of the crusaders. In a desperate attempt to try to bring an end to the senselessness of the fighting, Francis courageously (or, some might think, foolishly) set out across enemy lines in order to meet with the Sultan of Egypt, Malik-al-Kamil, who led the Muslim forces. Surprisingly, when Francis was apprehended by Muslim soldiers as he crossed enemy lines, they did not kill him on the spot. When Francis asked to see the Sultan, they, perhaps in a state of disbelief, took Francis

---

[6] A contemplative life is one oriented towards reflection, meditation, and prayer so as to come to an ever-growing awareness of God's presence in one's life.

to see him. Francis explained to the Sultan the reasonableness and what he saw as the rightness of his own Christian faith. The Sultan respectfully listened. The Sultan also explained the reasonableness and what he saw as the rightness of his own Islamic faith. Francis respectfully listened. In short, the two men entered into a respectful dialogue with each other. Each was impressed by the sincerity and genuine goodness of the other. While neither man adopted the faith of the other, they both left forever changed as a result of their meeting and with a new found respect for the faith of the other.

When Francis returned to Assisi from the Fifth Crusade, he was in an increasingly poor state of health. In addition to chronic illness, Francis also suffered deeply personal disappointments during the last years of his life. His group of followers had grown exponentially throughout Europe and, with confirmation of their Rule by the pope in 1223, had become officially known as the Order of Lesser Brothers (Friars Minor). But not all members of the Order embraced the same vision of absolute poverty as did Francis. Some friars wished to take a more practical and traditional approach to the ownership of property. Desiring to serve better the needs of the Church, they saw it as practical to be able to own certain things, such as churches, houses, and books. Given such a perceived abandonment of his ideal of absolute poverty, Francis felt betrayed and increasingly isolated in his own Order.

*Monastery of San Damiano*

In 1224 he retreated for prayer to the remote Mount La Verna, some 80 miles from Assisi. Questioning his own faithfulness to God's call in his life, Francis had a very intense spiritual experience on the mountain. Here Francis had a vision of the crucified Christ and he himself received the wounds of Christ, also known as the stigmata. While historians have debated just exactly what had happened on Mount La Verna and the nature of his wounds, the marks he exhibited clearly were meant to indicate that Francis had completely conformed his life to that of Jesus Christ.

By 1225, Francis was almost entirely blind. Yet it was during this period, as he was convalescing at the Monastery of San Damiano, that Francis composed the *Canticle of the Creatures,* the famous hymn in which he praised and thanked the God whom he had encountered through the wonder and beauty of creation. He eventually added a praise to God in which he described the blessings experienced by those who strive for peace and reconciliation. As he lay dying, Francis sang all of these praises and added yet another praise for "Sister Death." Francis died just outside of the Portiuncula on October 4, 1226.

Clare kept Francis' vision alive for another quarter century. Although she had to accept the regulations of a strict cloister (that is, never being allowed to leave the Monastery of San Damiano) in the late 1220's and was pressed by the pope to accept the ownership of property to support the operations of San Damiano, she continued to argue for the values of poverty and simple living. She finally was able to obtain confirmation of her own *Rule of Life* shortly before her death at San Damiano on August 11, 1253.

## MAJOR ASPECTS OF FRANCIS AND CLARE'S WORLDVIEW AND SPIRITUALITY

Having taken a brief look at some of the major events in the life of Francis and Clare, we can begin to identify some of the key elements of their distinctive worldview and spirituality. We will look at Francis and Clare's 1) emphasis on Jesus as the greatest example of God's love and humility, 2) attitude towards ownership and possession, 3) identification with the suffering of Jesus, and 4) manner of seeing God revealed in the world.

## EMPHASIS ON JESUS AS EXAMPLE OF GOD'S LOVE AND HUMILITY

Francis and Clare placed great emphasis on the love and humility of God. Perhaps you have heard God described as a God of love before, but you may be wondering how God can be described as being humble. For Francis and Clare, Jesus was the ultimate example of God's love and humility, for Jesus is not simply a holy man, but God who has become human. Christians refer to the event of God becoming human as the Incarnation (a term that will be discussed in more detail later). The belief that the God of the universe would lower himself to assume our "humanity and fragility"[7] in the person of Jesus struck Francis and Clare to their core and led Francis and Clare to reflect upon the significance of such an occurrence. Francis and Clare believed that God's choice to live among us in the person of Jesus demonstrated the great love that God has for humankind as well as God's great humility. Francis was so struck by the significance of the Incarnation that he wished to recreate the scene of Jesus' birth. Therefore, he staged what is thought to be the first living nativity scene near the small town of Greccio, Italy, in 1223. Here in a cave Francis brought together all of the sights, sounds, and smells of the manger scene of Jesus' birth as depicted in the Gospel of Luke. This reenactment helped Francis and all those gathered to reflect upon God's great love and humility as demonstrated by God's willingness to become human in the form of a vulnerable baby born into the lowly circumstances of a stable. Francis and Clare's emphasis on the love and humility of God would also affect other aspects of their spirituality, as will be seen below.

---

[7] Francis of Assisi, *Later Admonition and Exhortation*, FA:ED I, line 4, 46.

## Attitude towards Ownership and Possession

An important aspect of Francis and Clare's worldview was their attitude towards ownership and possession. As has been seen, Francis and Clare both rejected all forms of ownership and embraced lives of complete poverty. Francis turned his back on a comfortable merchant-class lifestyle to embrace a simple beggar's life without material possessions. For her part, Clare absolutely insisted that she and her sisters living in the Monastery of San Damiano would own absolutely nothing. There were a number of reasons that Francis and Clare desired to live lives devoid of all ownership.

First, Francis and Clare believed that ultimately everything belonged to God because God was the Creator and ultimate source of all. We humans are simply enjoying that which God has granted us to enjoy: things are not ours.

Secondly, through their own lives Francis and Clare wanted to reflect God's own generous self-giving love that had been displayed in a special way through creation, the Incarnation, and in the sending of his Spirit.

Thirdly, Francis and Clare wanted to be just like Jesus, who had been born into conditions of poverty in a stable and who had lived a poor life detached from ownership.

Fourthly, Francis and Clare wanted to break down societal barriers that separated them from the poor and marginalized, among whom God was in a special way to be found, and to use their resources to help those in most need.

Lastly, Francis and Clare wanted to distance themselves from all that might interfere with relationships—relationships with creation and other people but especially their relationships with God. Francis in particular held that the desire to possess (or to appropriate) for oneself led not only to seeing oneself as separate from the rest of creation and but also to conflict with others. The desire to possess also reflected a turning inward toward the self and a failure to recognize that, ultimately, all belongs to the sovereign and absolute God. In short, for Francis, the drive to possess or appropriate for oneself resulted in a failure to recognize that God alone is God and, thus, to a disrupted relationship with God.[8]

### A Deeper Understanding of Ownership and Possession

Francis encouraged his followers to live without anything of their own. For Francis, the concept of ownership or possession applied not only to material goods but also to attitudes. Thus, one could think about ownership and possession not only in a material sense but also in an attitudinal sense. This latter form of ownership or possession could involve stubbornly holding onto having things one's own way, consistently wanting to be "right," holding oneself to be better or holier than others, or protectively guarding one's image, time, interests, worldview, and positions. Francis called his followers to let go of these attitudes, all of which reflect a turning in towards oneself and away from life-giving relationships with God, others, and creation (See Francis of Assisi, *The Admonitions*, XI and XIV, 133-134, and Leclerc, *The Song of the Dawn*, 63).

## Identification with the Suffering of Jesus

Francis and Clare were struck not only by God becoming human in the person of Jesus but by the suffering that Jesus endured in life. Again, Jesus' suffering and ultimate death were living examples of God's love and humility. Francis and Clare's deep appreciation for Jesus' suffering also led them to a particular approach to suffering in the world around them. Neither Francis nor Clare fled from suffering. Rather, they accepted it in their own lives and in the world around them as a means that could

---

[8] Eloi Leclerc, *The Song of the Dawn* (Chicago: Franciscan Herald Press, 1977), 10, 25, 44-46.

bring them closer to Jesus.⁹ For his part, Francis was overwhelmed by the outpouring of God's love and humility demonstrated in the crucifixion and wanted to follow Jesus by laying down his life in service to God's people even if this involved suffering. In fact, Francis so desired to become like Jesus by experiencing Jesus' suffering that he had just such an experience on Mount La Verna.

For her part, Clare spent much time contemplating Jesus on the cross. This contemplation led Clare to a deeper appreciation of God's love and humility and to the realization that she too was called to embrace a life of loving and humble service to others, which in fact often involved suffering. Through such self-sacrifice and service, Clare mirrored Jesus's own life. Francis and Clare's identification with Jesus' suffering also affected the way that they saw God revealed in the world.

> **GOD'S HUMILITY AND LOVE REVEALED THROUGH JESUS**
>
> In a letter Clare encourages Agnes of Prague, a noble woman who wished to follow Clare's form of life, to gaze upon the "mirror" of Jesus so as to recognize his great humility, poverty, and love:
> Look, I say, at the border of this mirror, that is, the poverty of Him
>    Who was placed in a manger and wrapped in swaddling clothes.
>    O marvelous humility!
>    O astonishing poverty!
>       The King of angels,
>          the Lord of heaven and earth,
>             is laid in a manger!
> Then reflect upon, at the surface of the mirror,
>    the holy humility, at least the blessed poverty,
>       the untold labors and punishments
>          that He endured for the redemption of the whole human race.
> Finally contemplate, in the depth of this same mirror
>    the ineffable charity that He chose
>       to suffer on the tree of the Cross
>          and to die there the most shameful kind of death.
>
> (*The Fourth Letter to Agnes of Prague*, in *Clare of Assisi: Early Documents - The Lady*, ed. Regis J. Armstrong [New York: New City Press, 2006], lines 19-23, 56).

---

⁹ For example, in his *Canticle of the Creatures*, Francis prays: "Praised be You, my Lord, through those who give pardon for Your love, and bear infirmity and tribulation. Blessed are those who endure in peace for by You, Most High, shall they be crowned" (FA:ED I, lines 10-11, 114).

## GOD REVEALED IN THE WORLD

Francis and Clare did not believe that God was distant and uninvolved with the things of the world. On the contrary, the fact that God became human in the person of Jesus demonstrated that God was very much present in the world. The person of Jesus also gave Francis and Clare insights into where God was to be found. As already discussed, Clare and Francis were particularly attentive to Jesus' humility, poverty, and suffering. This led Francis and Clare to come to the conclusion that God dwelled among the lowly, the poor, and the suffering of the world in a special way. This is where Francis and Clare often experienced God. Furthermore, a deep appreciation for God's goodness led Francis and Clare to look for God in the goodness and beauty of all of creation. In short, the beauty of creation reflected the beauty of the Creator. Francis and Clare did not see themselves as separated from the rest of creation but as integrally linked to it. Relationships—with God, with others, with all of creation—were very important for Francis and Clare and seen as interrelated. God was to be found in relationships.

We have looked at the lives of Francis and Clare and at some of the major components of their worldview and spirituality. We will now turn to see how the Franciscan Intellectual Tradition developed these central themes from the lives of these great spiritual figures.

## QUESTIONS FOR REFLECTION AND DISCUSSION:

1. What aspects of the lives of Francis and Clare most struck you? Why?
2. How would you describe Francis' experience of conversion? What experiences of conversion have you experienced in your own life?
3. Francis heard Jesus' voice speaking to him from the crucifix in the Church of San Damiano? How might God speak to us today?
4. Francis and Clare were committed to generous lives devoid of ownership in every sense of the word (possession in a material sense and possession in an attitudinal sense [i.e., stubbornly holding onto one's own image, positions, interests, opinions, and worldview]). What do you think about this commitment? What practical purpose might it have served?
5. Where do you look for God? How is God revealed to you in your life?

# Chapter 2 – A Tradition Develops: Main Figures and Key Characteristics

Why are the lives of Francis and Clare important in our own world? How has the significance of their lives been explained and passed down to us? This chapter explores the Franciscan Intellectual Tradition, the "bridge" between the lives of Francis and Clare and our own world. First, we will look at what we mean by the term "intellectual tradition." Then we will examine the development, main figures, and key characteristics of the Franciscan Intellectual Tradition. These characteristics center on the Franciscan understanding of God, creation, and Jesus and are very much interrelated.

## What Is an Intellectual Tradition?

In the context of Christian theology, an intellectual tradition is a particular way of understanding and explaining important aspects of Christianity and the Christian view of the world.[10] In the Catholic Church's history, there have been three important intellectual traditions that have influenced many people for centuries: the Augustinian Tradition, the Thomistic Tradition, and the Franciscan Tradition. The Augustinian Tradition has its roots in the life of St. Augustine (354-430) and very much emphasizes human dependence on God's grace (or God sharing God's life with us) for our salvation and the manner in which the human person mirrors the Trinity, or the three distinct ways we experience the one God.[11i] The Thomistic (or Dominican) Tradition grew from the distinctive philosophical perspectives of the scholar St. Thomas Aquinas (1225-1274), a member of the religious order founded by St. Dominic (1170-1221). Some key elements of the Thomistic Tradition are the manner in which it emphasizes the oneness of God's nature, the distinctive difference between God and creation, human sin

---

[10] Intellectual traditions within Christianity tend to be academic in orientation and involve developing philosophical and theological ideas.

[11] The concept of the "Trinity" will be explored in more detail later as we look at specific aspects of the Franciscan Intellectual Tradition.

as the motivating factor leading to the Incarnation, the important role of the Church in making God present through the proclamation of the Word and the celebration of the sacraments[12], and the compatibility of faith and reason in leading us to God.[13] Since the 1800s, the Thomistic tradition has served as the dominant framework used to explain much of Church teaching. Some of the ways the Franciscan Tradition differs from its approach will be noted in the discussion below.

## ORIGINS OF THE FRANCISCAN INTELLECTUAL TRADITION

Although Francis did not originally plan on having a group of followers, many people were so inspired by his example that they decided to live a life following in his footsteps in order to draw closer to God. As has been pointed out earlier, Francis called those men who followed him "brothers" (or "friars"). These friars eventually became a religious community approved by the pope called the Order of Lesser Brothers (Friars Minor). Not long after Francis' death in 1226, some of these friars began to study at some of the great universities of Europe, such as the universities at Paris, Oxford, and Cambridge, in order to prepare themselves for ministry (or service) in the Church. However, they brought with them a distinctive way of viewing and understanding the Christian tradition, a way shaped by their own Franciscan way of life and the living example of St. Francis. This led them to put their own "spin" on the way they understood the Bible and the Tradition (the teachings that had been passed down) of the Church. The followers of St. Dominic were doing much the same thing at this time.[14] Very quickly, both Dominicans and Franciscans were not simply students at the universities, but holding important teaching posts there. Together, these Franciscan and Dominican scholars contributed greatly to a systematic way of approaching, explaining, and understanding the Christian faith that we call Scholasticism, which was dominant at the universities of the time. There were three main characteristics of Scholasticism.

First, Scholasticism was very deeply rooted in the philosophy of Aristotle (384-322 BC).[ii] Up to this point in the Church's history,

---

[12] Sacraments are rituals of the Church though which we encounter God in a special way.

[13] J.A. Weisheipl. "Thomism." *New Catholic Encyclopedia.* 2nd ed., 2002

[14] St. Francis and St. Dominic were contemporaries. Followers of both Francis and Dominic were referred to as "mendicants," which means "beggars." Rather than being secluded in monasteries, the followers of Francis and Dominic served the needs of those in cities and initially supported themselves through begging.

theology had usually been explained using the philosophy of Plato (428/7-348/7BC).[iii] During the time that Franciscans and Dominicans were becoming leading theologians at the great European universities, Latin translations of Aristotle and Islamic commentaries on his thought became available to Western scholars by way of Islamic scholars.[15] Because Aristotelian philosophy had a way to explain and categorize everything that possibly was, including that which was not physical but which the mind could conceive of, it was helpful to theologians, who began to use Aristotelian concepts to explain the Christian faith.

A second characteristic of Scholasticism was its use of the *Sentences* of Peter Lombard. The *Sentences* were a systematic collection of the main teachings of the Church that provided a convenient basis for scholars in the Scholastic movement to explore theological topics.

A third characteristic of Scholasticism was the dialectical method. The dialectical method was a very methodical, logical way of exploring issues within the Christian faith. A question would be posed and the various pros and cons of issues it raised were explored before coming to a firm conclusion as to what the fitting answer to the question should be.[16]

Why is the Scholastic method of exploring questions about God important? Because both the Franciscan and Dominican traditions expressed themselves using this method. While both the Franciscan and Dominican traditions applied the Scholastic method, scholars of these two mendicant orders arrived at significantly different conclusions, as will be seen.

## Main Figures and Key Characteristics of the Franciscan Intellectual Tradition

There were two leading scholars among the Franciscans who were especially vital to the development of the Franciscan Intellectual Tradition: St. Bonaventure (1221-1274)[iv] and Blessed John Duns Scotus (1266-1308).[v] While these two thinkers explored issues relating to the sacraments, sin, and redemption,[17] it is the way they came to understand God, creation, and Jesus that is most significant for us here in our exploration of the Franciscan Intellectual Tradition. Three important

---

[15] Kenan B. Osborne, *The Franciscan Intellectual Tradition: Tracing Its Origins and Identifying Its Central Components*. Franciscan Heritage Series, vol. 1 (St. Bonaventure, NY: Franciscan Institute, 2003), 11.

[16] Osborne, *The Franciscan Intellectual Tradition*, 11-12.

[17] Osborne, *The Franciscan Intellectual Tradition*, 13-14. Redemption refers to the manner in which humankind is brought into a renewed relationship with God.

conclusions will be made about the Franciscan Intellectual Tradition's distinctive emphases regarding God, creation, and Jesus:

1) The Franciscan Intellectual Tradition emphasizes God as a relationship of overflowing love and goodness who is entirely free.

2) The Franciscan Intellectual Tradition emphasizes that creation is a reflection of a loving, good, and free Creator, who is in relationship with his creation and who willed into being every individual, unique creature that exists.

3) The Franciscan Intellectual Tradition emphasizes that the Incarnation of the Son of God in the person of Jesus was a free and intentional expression of God's self-giving love and humility and an affirmation of humanity's dignity and goodness.

## Who is God?

As you can see, we are not starting out with an easy question! In order to explore the Franciscan understanding of God, we have to go back to the fundamental Christian belief in the Trinity, a belief that is expressed in the Nicene Creed. This Creed is still the classic statement of Christian faith; you may be familiar with it, as it is part of the Sunday worship of the Catholic Church and several other churches as well. The Creed explains that there are three distinguishable ways that we experience the one God. The three ways that we experience God are most often termed "persons": Father, Son, and Holy Spirit. [vi]

The Trinity is a concept around which we will never be able to fully wrap our minds. However, we do not need to experience anxiety and worry over this; the Trinity is a not a heavenly jig-saw puzzle that we have to "figure out," but a mystery and a relationship in which we ourselves are invited to participate. You can even think of the Trinity as a dance that we are called to enter without worrying about missteps.

Christians have been have been reflecting on God's life for nearly two millennia. While the Bible never mentions the Trinity in a technical sense, it does refer to three distinguishable ways that Christians experience and relate to God: Father, Son, and Holy Spirit. For example, St. Paul tells us: "May the grace of our Lord Jesus Christ (the Son), the love of God (the Father), and the fellowship of the Holy Spirit be with you" (2 Cor.

13:14). Francis, too, refers to the three ways we experience God when he tells Christians how blessed we are to have a loving "Father" in heaven; "a brother," Jesus, who shares our humanity; and a "spouse," the Holy Spirit, to whom our souls are united.[18]

As time went on, Christians began to see that the term "Trinity" does not simply describe the ways in which God relates to us, but in fact describes a relationship *within* God. God's very being is relational, a dynamic of love that exists between the three persons in the one God. What is important for understanding the Franciscan Intellectual Tradition is whether we stress the "three" or the "one" in this phrase "three persons in one God." Franciscans thinkers, following Bonaventure, have tended to stress the "three" – that our understanding of God is not that of a solitary "unmoved mover" (as in the philosophy of Aristotle), but rather is that of a dynamic relationship of love. Significantly, Bonaventure started out by describing God as Supreme Good.[19] He went on to ask what this means. Since goodness by its very nature is self-giving, he concluded that God, the Supreme Good, must be total self-giving love. God must be Love because love is the ultimate good. Therefore, while God (the ultimate reality) is one, there must be some distinction of persons within God by means of which God can literally be a relationship of love. Bonaventure then argued that the greatest love is when the love between two persons is shared with a third. Thus, Bonaventure concluded that there must be a plurality of three persons within God.[20] Many of us may have heard the statement from the Bible, "God is love" (1 John 4:16). Often we interpret the statement that "God is love" to mean that God is *loving*. While this is certainly true, for Bonaventure the significance of God being love went beyond the fact that God is loving. According to Bonaventure, God is not just *loving* but is *Love* itself.

Again, you need not despair if you are still somewhat confused after this exploration of the Trinity. As stated earlier, the Trinity is mystery in that it is a reality that can never be fully understood by our human minds. What is most important for an exploration of the Franciscan Intellectual Tradition is that Bonaventure saw God as a loving relationship of three persons, a relationship whose love overflows into all of creation.

---

[18] Francis of Assisi, *Later Admonitions and Exhortations*, FA:ED I, lines 49-56, 48-49.

[19] Bonaventure, *Soul's Journey into God*, in *The Soul's Journey into God, The Tree of Life, The Life of St. Francis*, ed. Ewert Cousins. History of Christian Spirituality Series. (Mahwah, NJ: Paulist, 1978), chap. 6, section 2, 102-4.

[20] For Bonaventure's full exploration of the Trinity, see Zachary Hayes, trans. Works of St. Bonaventure. *Disputed Questions on the Mystery of the Trinity*, (St. Bonaventure, NY: Franciscan Institute Publications, 2000).

God wants to freely share the love that constitutes God's very nature with others ... and that is us! While Bonaventure emphasized God as loving relationship of three persons, the Dominican scholar Thomas Aquinas emphasized God's oneness and transcendence (that is, "otherness").[21] And so we can see that one distinctive aspect of the Franciscan Intellectual Tradition is understanding God in terms of a loving relationship (between persons) who is in an intimate loving relationship with his creation.

For his part, Duns Scotus, too, emphasized God as loving relationship. But a key aspect of Scotus' understanding of God is God's unbridled freedom. According to Scotus, God was not and is not required to do anything. God does not get backed into corners and become forced to act by circumstances. Rather, God always acts out of loving freedom. This concept will become particularly important below when we explore the Franciscan understanding of why God became human in the person of Jesus Christ.

**Key point to remember: The Franciscan Intellectual Tradition emphasizes God as a relationship of overflowing love and goodness who is entirely free.**

### GOD'S OVERFLOWING LOVE

> Bonaventure described God as "fountain fullness" of love. Like a fountain that overflows, God's own infinitely self-giving love (that which God is by God's very nature) overflows into all of creation, including and especially humankind (see Bonaventure's *Breviloquium* 1.3.7).

## CREATION: WHY IS THERE SOMETHING INSTEAD OF NOTHING?

The Franciscan understanding of the relationship between God and creation is another distinctive feature of the Franciscan Intellectual Tradition. According to Bonaventure, creation flowed freely from the love of the Trinity and was not something separate from it.

---

[21] Osborne, *Franciscan Intellectual Tradition*, 57, 59-60.

For Bonaventure, creation not only was the result of an outpouring of God's love but also served as the backdrop for God's most profound demonstration of self-giving love: the Incarnation, that is, God becoming human in the person of Jesus. In describing the significance of creation, Bonaventure referred to three ways creation is related to God: creation came forth from God, creation reflects God, and creation is intended to return to God.[22] First, according to Bonaventure, all creation came forth from God through the Son of God[23], the second person of the Trinity who has existed from all time.

But secondly, because all things have come into being through God the Son, all of creation reflects God in some way.[vii] In discussing the way all of creation reflects God, Bonaventure spoke of the "Book of Creation." He was not referring to any book of the Bible or to any other literal book but to created things themselves. According to Bonaventure, "reading" this "book" by contemplating the wonders of creation is a very real way that we can come to know God.[24] By describing creation in this manner, Bonaventure emphasized the goodness of creation and the concept of sacramentality, the belief that we can come to know and encounter God through the world around us.[25] Finally, Bonaventure taught that all of creation is being brought to completion and led back into God through

---

[22] Bonaventure used the term "emanation" to describe all of creation coming forth from God, the term "exemplarity" to describe how all of creation reflects or reveals God, and "consummation" to describe creation returning to and being brought to fullness in God.

[23] The second person of the Trinity is the Son. Another term used to describe the second person of the Trinity is the "Word." Why? What do we do with words? What do words allow us to do? We express or communicate ourselves with our words. Therefore, the Son is God's Word, that is, God's self-expression or self-communication. Bonaventure called the Son the "Eternal Art" of the Father, for in this Eternal Word, God expresses totally everything God wants to do (*Soul's Journey into God* 1.3). It is precisely this total self-expression of God, the eternal Word or Son, that Christians believe became human in the person of Jesus. In describing the Incarnation of the Son (or Word) of God, the Gospel of John states, "In the beginning was the Word, . . and the Word was God. He was in the beginning with God. All things came into being through him, and without him not one thing came into being. … And the Word became flesh and dwelt among us and we have seen his glory" (Jn. 1:1-3, 14).

[24] Bonaventure referred to "three" books by which we can come to know God. The "Book of Creation" is described in this chapter. According to Bonaventure, one can come to know God by "reading" or contemplating the wonders of creation. Bonaventure also referred to the "Book of Life." This "book" can be found in one's innermost self where God speaks to a person in the quiet of his or her heart. Finally, there is the Book of Scriptures or the Gospels. God is revealed to us through the Scriptures and in a special way through the Gospels. We come to know God more intimately by "reading" all three books, which together reveal God to us.

[25] The concept of sacramentality will be addressed in more detail in chapter 3.

God's Son, through whom, as has been pointed out, all creation was made. In this sense, it is not just humankind that is being "saved." Rather, all creation is being saved.

In short, through his understanding that creation came forth from God, reveals God, and is now being brought back into God, Bonaventure very much emphasized the close connection between God and creation as well as the sacredness and goodness of creation as an expression of God's love that can lead us to God.

Like Bonaventure, Duns Scotus also saw creation as a free expression of God's love. According to Scotus, who emphasized God's freedom, nothing had to exist or be unless a loving God willed it into being. Thus all things, by the very fact that they exist, are gifts of God. Perhaps one of Scotus' most significant contributions to our understanding of creation is his notion of *haecceitas*, a Latin word meaning "thisness." To understand Scotus' concept of *haecceitas,* we need to contrast it with the four categories found within the philosophy of Aristotle who was mentioned earlier in this chapter.[26] When describing an object, Aristotelian philosophy emphasizes the "substance" of a being. For Aristotle, the substance of a being is that quality that made a being what it is. For example, the substance that makes one a human being is that one is a rational animal. Our rational animal nature is our "substance." Within Aristotelian philosophy, the substance of a being is the most important and most basic characteristic of that being. On the other hand, according to Aristotelian philosophy, "accidents," or characteristics such as shape, color, height, and width, distinguish beings in relationship to other beings of the same substance and constitute the least important category for describing an object. For example, within the framework of Aristotelian philosophy, our substance as rational animals is more important to our being than any characteristics (that is, "accidents") that distinguish one individual from another other: such as our gender, race, etc. Scotus rejected this stress on the importance of substance over accidents. More simply put, Scotus saw the individuality of beings and their relationship to one another as being more significant than overall, general groupings. This had important implications for Scotus' understanding of God and God's creation. For Scotus, God did not will certain categories/genera/species of creatures and then decide to create individual creatures within those broad categories. For example, God did not will to create humankind in general and then decide to make individual humans. Rather, according to Scotus, God lovingly and individually wills each and every creature

---

[26] These Aristotelian categories were emphasized within the Dominican Intellectual Tradition.

into existence. Thus, every creature has *haecceitas*, that is, its own unique being, quality, value, worth, and purpose for existing—what Scotus referred to as the "dignity of particularity."[27] A particular tree's *haecceitas* is what makes that tree unlike any other in existence, one that has been individually and lovingly brought into existence by God. An individual person's *haecceitas* is that which makes that person uniquely him or her, again individually willed and lovingly brought into existence by God. God did not decide to create the human race and then to make you as a particular human individual. No, according to Scotus, God intentionally chose to create you, with all your uniqueness *to live in relationship with other unique persons*. Consequently, as a unique human being, you contribute to the makeup of the human race. Again, according to Scotus, the individual in relationship to others is more important than general categories, not vice versa.

This emphasis on the *haeccetias* of each creature, in contrast to an emphasis on a creature's "substance" that it shares with every other creature like it, is one way the Franciscan approach to creation is different from that of other intellectual traditions. There are also other ways the Franciscan understanding of creation differs from that found in other traditions. Theologians such as Thomas Aquinas, again basing their understanding of creation on the philosophy of Aristotle, emphasized creation as caused by God, as something different and distinct from God (i.e., different in being), and as an expression of God's power.[28] Bonaventure and Scotus, as has been seen, saw creation as flowing from and very much connected to a free and loving God by its very being. Thus, they emphasized creation as an expression and reflection of God's goodness that can, in fact, help to lead us to God, the Creator and Source of all goodness. In addition, as we have seen, Scotus emphasized the uniqueness of each creature individually willed into existence by God. A distinctive component of the Franciscan Intellectual Tradition is the manner in which it emphasizes the goodness of creation, the relationship God has with creation, creation as a reflection of God that can in fact be a means by which we encounter God, and the uniqueness and value of every creature.

**Key point to remember: The Franciscan Intellectual Tradition emphasizes that creation is a reflection of a loving, good, and free Creator, who is in relationship with his creation and who willed into being every individual, unique creature that exists.**

---

[27] Daniel P. Horan, *Dating God: Live and Love in the Way of St. Francis* (Cincinnati: St. Anthony Messenger Press, 2012), 31.

[28] See, for example, Osborne, *Franciscan Intellectual Tradition*, 65.

### LIFE THROUGH DEATH

The "paschal mystery" lies at the heart of the Christian faith. Rooted in Jesus' own death and resurrection, this mystery is the belief that we come to *life* by passing through *death*. Jesus rose to glorious new life through his rising from the dead. We, too, one day will rise to new life after we have physically died. But the paschal mystery reflects yet another reality: It is through *dying* to ourselves (that is, looking beyond ourselves and our own wants and preferences) and giving of ourselves for the good of others that we find the real meaning of *life* (Lk 9:24). The paschal mystery also gives us the hope that "life" (growth, development, deeper relationships, and even joy) can come from the "small deaths" that we experience. In short, Jesus' own death and resurrection teach us that death, brokenness, and suffering do not get the final word in our lives.

### WHERE DOES JESUS FIT IN?

In many ways, this is an odd question to pose at this point, as the Franciscan understanding of God and creation actually begins with Jesus Christ. As noted earlier, Christians believe that Jesus is God, the eternal Son, who became human in the event referred to as the Incarnation in order to reveal who God truly is.[29] From the days of Francis' first encounter with the Cross of San Damiano, the person of Jesus was at the forefront of his imagination. It was the fact that Jesus freely poured out his life for us on the cross that most powerfully revealed for him that God is total, self-giving love. As he said in a prayer he taught his followers: "We adore you, Lord Jesus Christ, in all your churches throughout the world and we bless you, because by your holy cross you have redeemed the world."[30] Christians continue to celebrate this mystery of human salvation during Holy Week (the week leading up to Easter): that the significance of Jesus' entire life culminates in his passion (suffering), death, and resurrection.

But this mystery inevitably has led to questions that have surfaced in the field of Christology, the area of theology that explores our understanding of Jesus: *why* did God became human in the person of Jesus in the first place, and *why* did Jesus have to suffer on the cross? The

---

[29] "No one has ever seen God. It is God the only Son, who is close to the Father's heart, who has made him known" (John 1:18).

[30] Francis of Assisi, *The Testament*, FA:ED I, lines 4-5, 124-125.

Franciscan Intellectual Tradition offers its own distinctive answer to these questions.

For much of the history of the Church in the West, the explanation for why God became human focused on human sinfulness. This is not surprising, given key passages in the New Testament that undoubtedly shaped Francis' own imagination.[31] But did this mean that human sinfulness was the *only* reason why God became human? According to the dominant explanation given in the Middle Ages in the West, the answer to that question was *yes*. That answer was given in a work by a theologian named Anselm (1033-1109) in a work called *Why God became Human*,[32] and is called the satisfaction theory of the atonement (how human beings are again "made one" with God).[33] To understand Anselm's explanation, one has to know a little bit about medieval thinking.

According to medieval reasoning, if an offense is committed against a person, only someone of that person's dignity or higher could truly make up for the offense committed. That is, if person A commits an offense against person B, person A can only make up for that offense if person A is of a social status equal to or higher than that of person B. For example, in the medieval world, a serf could never truly make up for an offense he committed against a prince. The serf simply did not have any way to compensate the prince for the offense against him. And so, as Anselm's reasoning went, because God was infinitely greater than humankind, humankind could never satisfy the demands of God's justice in a way that would make up or set right the balance for all the sins human beings had committed. Because the only equal to God is God, only God could pay the price for the sin that had been committed by humankind and bring humankind back into right relationship with God. Yet there was a catch here. Because it was humankind that had sinned, justice required that it was humankind that had to pay the price. Thus, the only way that the sin could be atoned for (or made up for) was by God (the only one who could pay the price) to become human (the one who was required to pay the price). As noted above, this explanation that Jesus (as "God-man") had to offer his own life in order to bring humankind back into right relationship with God after human beings had sinned is called the "satisfaction theory." One implication of the satisfaction theory is that

---

[31] Such as Paul and John: "But God proves his love for us in that while we were still sinners Christ died for us" (Romans 5:8); "God's love was revealed among us in this way: . . . that God sent his Son to be the atoning sacrifice for our sins" (1 Jn: 9-10).

[32] In Latin, *Cur Deus Homo*. This work was written about a hundred years before the time of Francis.

[33] See Thomas P. Rausch, *Who Is Jesus?: An Introduction to Christology* (Collegeville, MN: Liturgical Press, 2003), 186-188.

God became human by default. Humankind through the poor exercise of freewill had messed things up by sinning so Jesus, God-become-human, had to bring humankind back into right relationship with God by paying the price of human sinfulness through sacrificing his life in a bloody, violent crucifixion.

However, unlike Anselm, Bonaventure and Scotus' explanations for why God became human were not focused on human sin and the idea that God became human by default. Rather, creation, the Incarnation, and the eventual sending of God's Spirit were all part of God's original design and were the natural result of the outpouring of God's infinitely generous love. Bonaventure emphasized that God sent his Son to become human because God, being true to his nature as self-giving Love, wished to crown the work of his creation by giving and uniting himself fully to that creation as a human being. In Bonaventure's system, Jesus and the Incarnation thus play a critical role in how he understood all creation as coming from, revealing, and returning to God. The Son, who *comes forth* from God and through whom all creation *came forth* into being, becomes part of that process himself by becoming human in the person of Jesus (John 1:3-3, 14). Furthermore, the Son who became incarnate was and continues to be the ultimate way that God has been *revealed* in the world.[viii]

Finally, it is through the Son becoming human and joining in creation that the process of the *return* of all creation to God began.[ix] For Bonaventure, the Incarnation was a deep expression of God's love that flowed from God's very nature, played a key function in the relationship between God and creation, and affirmed the goodness of humanity.[34]

> **JESUS, EXPRESSION OF GOD'S LOVE**
>
> "God comes to us in hiddenness; God hides in ordinary things and in Jesus. In the humility and poverty of Jesus we see that God does not stand over creation but bends down to lift us up into union with the divine. The cross is the most intense revelation of divine humility" (Ilia Delio, OSF, *The Humility of God: A Franciscan Perspective* [Cincinnati, OH: St. Anthony Messenger Press, 2005[)].

Scotus similarly held that, rather than serving as a reminder of human sin, the Incarnation underlined God's deep love freely given to humanity as well as humanity's inherent goodness and dignity. He reasoned that if the person of Christ is the greatest expression of God's love, then why

---

[34] Given the key role that the Incarnation plays in the Bonaventure's system of creation coming forth from, reflecting, and returning to God, Bonaventure held that the Incarnation points to the goodness not only of humanity but also of all of creation.

should it be dependent on something evil – human sinfulness – to exist? He concluded that the greatest expression of God's love did not happen only by default. Rather, in his infinite relationship of love, God willed first, before anything else, even before creating the world, to communicate God's self fully outside the Trinity – to another. God created the world so that God might fully communicate (or give) himself to that creation in the person of Jesus Christ.[35]

All of this does not mean that the Franciscan Intellectual Tradition does not take seriously the reality of human sin. It is not hard to look at history or the contemporary situation in our world to see that humankind does not always live up to its dignity as created in the image of God (Genesis 1:27). Bonaventure argued that humankind fails to live up to its dignity and is unable to recognize God's presence in the world because it is bent over in the self-centeredness of sin.[36] Because of sin, humankind needed something to straighten it up into its upright position again. This "something" was God's Son become human in the person of Jesus. Through his life, death, and resurrection, Jesus teaches us the full meaning of humanity is recognized in self-giving love. He teaches us how to walk upright (vs. being bent over in the self-centeredness of sin) and how to live fully as children of God. One way Jesus accomplished this was through his death. Let's be clear: humankind determined that Jesus should die. Jesus was killed by the sinfulness of humans who perceived Jesus and his message of God's love to be a threat to their own control and power, not because a price had to be paid to satisfy an offended God. Jesus did not perpetuate the deadly cycle of violence by responding to hatred with more of the same. Jesus' response to the hatred and violence of the world was a self-giving love that gave that hatred and violence a place to die. Through his death, Jesus expressed the ultimate depth of God's love for humankind, a love originally demonstrated through the Incarnation itself. Through his death, he also taught us that that the real meaning of life is to be found in giving of ourselves for the good of others (Luke 9:23-24). It was this self-sacrificing, self-giving love that brought humankind into a renewed relationship with God and that so moved Francis and Clare to the point that they wanted to demonstrate the same generous love through their own lives.

One's understanding of why God became human in the person of Jesus affects one's understanding of salvation. We often banter about the word "salvation" without actually considering what it means. From

---

[35] "He (Jesus Christ) is the image of the invisible God, the first-born of all creation; for in him all things in heaven and earth were created. . . . All things have been created through him and for him" (Col 1:15-16).

[36] *The Soul's Journey into God,* 1.7, 62.

a Christian perspective, salvation, in a very basic sense, refers to union or being in relationship with God, which can be experienced to a degree in this world and more fully in the next. It is this relationship that saves one from meaninglessness, emptiness, and all of the things that hold us bound in our lives. If one believes that Jesus became human in order to pay a price to appease a disgruntled God, it would be Jesus' death that would achieve salvation for humankind. The Franciscan understanding of salvation is much broader. According to Franciscan theology, it was not just Jesus' death that brought salvation to humankind. It is everything about Jesus' life[37], culminating in his death and resurrection, that effected humankind's salvation. It is through his entire being that Jesus brings us into union with God.[38]

This would be a good time to bring together what has been stated so far. The Franciscan Intellectual Tradition understands the Incarnation of God in the person of Jesus to have been part of God's original design and the result of God's inherent self-giving and loving nature. According to the Franciscan Intellectual Tradition, the Incarnation of God in the person of Jesus was not an afterthought on the part of God or the unintended result of humankind having sinned. Rather the Incarnation is seen as the ultimate way that God has revealed himself and freely given his love to humanity and all of creation. In short, God became human primarily because of who *God* is, not because of what *humankind* had done.

The Franciscan Intellectual Tradition's understanding of the Incarnation differs somewhat from the understanding that the Dominican (or Thomistic) Intellectual Tradition based on the theology of Thomas Aquinas would offer. According to Thomas, the reason for creation was very much separate from the reason for the Incarnation.[39] Thomas viewed creation as an expression of the power and distinct supremacy of God, an expression that demonstrated the gulf between God and all of God's creatures. In contrast, within the Franciscan Tradition, creation is intimately related to God, is an expression of the overflowing love of God, and serves as the perfect backdrop for God's greatest expression of love: the Incarnation. Furthermore, in Thomas' theology, God became human in the person of Jesus to pay a price for human sin and to set the scales of justice into proper balance as they had been in at the

---

[37] One is reminded of how moved Francis was by God's humility and love expressed by God giving himself to humanity as a vulnerable baby, a scene which Francis recreated at Greccio.

[38] Hayes, *Christ, Word of God and Exemplar of Humanity*, 2.

[39] Kenan B. Osborne, "The Franciscan Intellectual Tradition: What Is It? Why Is It Important?," *AFCU Journal* 5, no. 1 (2008): 15.

beginning of creation.[40] In contrast, as has been seen, the Franciscan Intellectual Tradition focuses on the Incarnation as an expression of God's overflowing love and not just the result of human sinfulness. Furthermore, the Franciscan Intellectual Tradition stresses the manner in which the Incarnation points to the goodness of both humanity and the rest of creation, both of which are being brought back into union with God through Jesus, God's Son become human. In short, the Franciscan Intellectual Tradition in a distinctive way emphasizes the goodness and love of God, the goodness of humanity, and the goodness of creation. As will be seen in the next chapter, these emphases can have tremendous modern implications for how we understand our relationship with God, one another, and the world.

**Key Point to Remember: The Franciscan Intellectual Tradition emphasizes that the Incarnation of the Son of God in the person of Jesus was a free and intentional expression of God's self-giving love and humility and an affirmation of humanity's dignity and goodness.**

## What Happened to the Franciscan Intellectual Tradition?

One might be led to ask what happened to the influence of the Franciscan Intellectual Tradition, especially as it was shaped and expressed by Bonaventure and Scotus. Because of the Franciscan presence and influence at the great European universities, non-Franciscans were also exposed to the Franciscan Intellectual Tradition, which became an important way of expressing the Catholic faith. Even as late as the 16th Century, the Franciscan Intellectual Tradition continued to have a significant impact within the Church. Documents from the Council of Trent, a council of Catholic bishops held during the 16th Century to respond to the Protestant Reformation, drew upon both the Franciscan and Dominican schools of thought in the formulation of its documents. Since the Renaissance[41] and the Council of Trent, however, the Catholic Church increasingly turned to the Dominican, Thomistic Intellectual Tradition to express its tenets of faith. The Franciscan Intellectual Tradition took on what might be seen a gradually diminishing role.

---

[40] Osborne, "The Franciscan Intellectual Tradition," *AFCU Journal*, 16.

[41] The Renaissance was a period (roughly 14th to 17th Centuries) bridging the medieval and modern periods. Characteristics of the Renaissance include a renewed interest in the classic expressions of Roman and Greek culture, an emphasis on the human person, and great artistic achievements.

By the Age of Enlightenment of the 18th Century[42], Scholasticism in general was falling out of favor in wider philosophical circles, although the Thomistic (Dominican) Tradition retained its pivotal influence within the world of Catholic theology as the primary philosophical tool for expressing the Catholic faith. By the late 1800's, however, Franciscan scholars set to work to retrieve their distinctive Intellectual Tradition. Work began to be done to publish critical editions of the works of its leading figures, such as Bonaventure and Scotus, making their thought available; this work continued in the early 20th century. Nevertheless, the documents of the Second Vatican Council, called in the 1960's in order to renew the Catholic Church in the modern world, make no specific reference to the Franciscan Intellectual Tradition in expressing the Church's faith for today.[43] The omission is telling. A tradition that had so much to offer the renewal of the Church and the modern world in general was ignored. However, that same Council urged religious orders to retrieve their distinctive "charisms" or spiritual gifts: to rediscover the animating spirit and fundamental insights of their founders and translate these in terms of our contemporary world.[44] Since 1970, Franciscans have made a major effort to immerse themselves in the writings of Francis and Clare and, more recently, the works of major Franciscan thinkers. Therefore, we are in a much better position than we were before the Second Vatican Council to ask: What exactly is it that the Franciscan Intellectual Tradition has to offer us today? It is to that question that we will turn in the next chapter.

## QUESTIONS FOR REFLECTION AND DISCUSSION:

1. What aspect of the Franciscan Intellectual Tradition has struck you the most?
2. What images do you use to describe God? How would you describe God in general? Does your description emphasize God's justice or God's love? How might the Franciscan approach to understanding God be different from or similar to the understanding of God you have had up to this point in your

---

[42] The Enlightenment is noted for its rejection of earlier (and, in particular, religious) ways of understanding the world as well as its emphasis on the use of reason to arrive at knowledge.

[43] For more information on what has happened to the Franciscan Intellectual Tradition over the centuries, see Osborne, "The Franciscan Intellectual Tradition," *AFCU Journal*, 7-10.

[44] Decree *Perfectae Caritatis*, 2.

life? What insights into understanding God does the Franciscan Intellectual Tradition provide you?

3. How would you describe your relationship with creation? Do you see your relationship with God as having any effect on your relationship with creation (and vice versa)?

4. Who do you understand Jesus to be? What explanation might you give for why God became human in the person of Jesus? How has the Franciscan Intellectual Tradition influenced your understanding of the significance of Jesus and your explanation as to why God became human?

# Chapter 3 – So What?: Why the Franciscan Intellectual Tradition Matters

We have seen how the life of Francis and Clare served as the foundation of the development of an intellectual tradition that emphasizes that
1) God is a God of overflowing love,
2) God is revealed through the goodness of creation, and
3) Jesus is the ultimate expression of God's love and humility who affirms humanity's goodness.

But what does that tradition have to offer us living in the twenty-first century? How might the Tradition address some of the more pressing issues of our world? How does it speak to our day-to-day concerns? This chapter will consider a number of different ways that the Franciscan Intellectual Tradition might really affect how we view and understand the world around us. Here we will explore how the Franciscan Intellectual Tradition

1) expands our image of God and understanding of Jesus,
2) offers insights into addressing an impending environmental crisis,
3) presents a positive understanding of morality based on responding to God's generous love,
4) proposes an attitude towards ownership and possession that promotes healthy relationships,
5) leads to a growth in respect for the dignity of all life, especially human life,
6) provides insights into living in a world of religious diversity and into finding a genuine peace through a sense of our connectedness with one another,
7) promotes a disposition of gratitude and joy that can contribute much to our lives today, and finally,
8) offers a concept of contingency (the belief that the only thing that has to be is God) that helps us to thrive in a world of great change.

As we will see, the insights that the Franciscan Intellectual Tradition offers into these various topics are often interrelated. This chapter will challenge you to consider how the Franciscan Intellectual Tradition relates to your own life, affects your own understanding of the world, and offers insights into humanity's deepest concerns.

## GOD IMAGES: WHO DO I UNDERSTAND GOD TO BE?

Who is God? What images do we use to describe God? Our answers to these questions are foundational to our approach to other issues examined in this chapter. Sometimes images used to describe God evoke a distant god who is to be feared or a god who is waiting for us to make a misstep so that he can punish us. In contrast to these images, Francis' heart was very much moved by the love and humility of God. He could especially see evidence of God's love in the world all around him. Francis was particularly struck by the love and humility of God displayed in the Incarnation: the mighty God of the universe so much loved us that God wished to draw near to us by humbly becoming one of us.

As we have seen, as the Franciscan Intellectual Tradition developed in the years after Francis, Bonaventure emphasized God as a God of overflowing love and goodness.[45] Furthermore, Bonaventure also stressed the communitarian nature of God. Thus, the Franciscan Intellectual

---

[45] See Bonaventure, *Breviloquium* 1.3.7 and *Soul's Journey into God* 6.2.

Tradition offers us a way of understanding God that may better reflect our experience of God than do images of a god who is primarily distant and to be feared. Few people want to be involved with a god who uses fear and the threat of punishment to coerce us into relationship and into certain forms of behavior. In contrast, the Franciscan Intellectual Tradition emphasizes God as a *relationship* of love and as a God who desires nothing more than for us to enter into full union with that life-giving relationship. Importantly, God draws us into that relationship through love and mercy rather than through fear and judgment.

This is an image of God that some people may find better corresponds to the true nature of God than images they have focused on in the past. Significantly, this emphasis on God as a relationship of love also points to the importance of relationships – with God, others, ourselves, and all creation – in our own lives. The Franciscan understanding of God might help one to recognize more fully the value of all relationships in his or her life and, thereby, to enter more deeply into relationship with God, who is seen as evoking love rather than fear.

**Franciscan Focus: God is not a God of fear and arbitrary laws. Rather, God is a God of love, humility, and relationship.**[x]

## JESUS: WHY DOES HE MATTER?

One's understanding of Jesus, who is God-become-human, is naturally connected to one's understanding of God. As noted above, for Francis, Jesus was the ultimate expression of God's love and humility. Francis was deeply moved by the infinite love displayed by the almighty God of the universe who so wanted to draw close to us that he, in an act of great humility, took upon himself our "humanity and frailty" by becoming a tiny infant.[46]

As we have seen in chapter 1, this great love and humility was driven home for Francis in his reenactment of the nativity scene at Greccio. God's love and humility were further emphatically demonstrated for Francis by Jesus' free giving of himself on the cross. As noted in Chapter 2, as the Franciscan Intellectual Tradition developed, Bonaventure and Scotus also emphasized Jesus as the greatest expression of God's goodness, love, and humility.

As also seen earlier, the Franciscan Intellectual Tradition's emphasis on Jesus as an expression of God's love becomes clear in its explanation for why God became human in the first place. The Tradition places more

---

[46] Francis of Assisi, *Later Admonition and Exhortation*, FA:ED I, line 4, 46.

emphasis on the belief that God became human in the person of Jesus Christ as a natural and free outpouring of God's love and goodness rather than on the belief that God became human just to settle some horrible debt resulting from human sin. While definitely recognizing the sinfulness of humanity, the Franciscan Intellectual Tradition emphasizes humanity's goodness as creatures whom God lovingly created in God's own image and to whom God wished to draw near through the person of Jesus. Again, the Franciscan Tradition emphasizes that God became human because of who *God* is, not because of what *humankind* did. Furthermore, as fully God and fully human, Jesus, the most vivid demonstration of God's deep love for us and desire to be in union with us, reveals to us who God is and who we are called to be. The Franciscan Tradition's emphasis on God's love as expressed through the Incarnation reminds us that we too, like Jesus, are called to be an incarnational people—that is, to "put flesh" on Gods' presence in the world— through living lives of self-sacrificing love.[47]

So far we have been looking at the Franciscan Intellectual Tradition's emphasis on Jesus as the ultimate expression of God's love. As noted above, Francis was also struck by how Jesus expressed God's great humility. Since God is the ultimate Source of all that is and is Lord of the universe, only a very humble God, would set aside God's own grandeur to become an infant born into the simplest and poorest of circumstances purely out of love for us. In the Franciscan Intellectual Tradition, God's own humility serves as a life-giving model for our own attitude towards pride and power. Rather than thinking of ourselves as over and above others, we are able to humbly recognize who we are in relationship to God.[48] All that we are is a gift from God and we are nothing apart from God. From a position of humility, one sees one's interrelatedness with others and the rest of creation. One also develops a special sensitivity for the marginalized and neglected who reveal the face of God to us, as lepers did for Francis.[xi] Humility, thus, becomes an essential component of right relationship with God, others, oneself, and creation.

In short, the Franciscan Intellectual Tradition can help us to come to a deeper understanding of the significance of who Jesus is. The emphasis

---

[47] As noted in chapter 1, Clare was struck by God's poverty, humility, and charity as expressed by Jesus Christ. Clare saw Jesus as a mirror that reflected the image of God to us. In looking in the mirror of Christ, Clare also saw the image of the person she was called to become.

[48] As noted earlier, Francis' followers were referred to as the "Lesser Brothers," a title which pointed to their own sense of humility before God and others (FA:ED I, *The Later Rule*, par. 1, 99). Today, male followers of Francis who profess vows of poverty, chastity, and obedience are referred to as "friars minor," a term with the same meaning and commitment to humility as "lesser brothers."

within the Franciscan Intellectual Tradition is on Jesus as an expression of God's love and humility and as a model of the people we are called to be.

**Franciscan Focus: Jesus is the ultimate expression of God's love and humility who brings us into relationship with God and the ultimate example of what it means to be fully human.**

### God's Generous Love

"The very life of God is one of goodness itself expressing itself generously, fully. God's desire to share goodness is expressed as creation. . . . Creation is fully understandable at the *birth of Jesus*. Here is the "missing link," always present, now visible . . . Christ is no alien in a strange universe: he was from the beginning the reason and the *Creator's blueprint for every particle of matter*, for all things visible and invisible, for everything and everyone...

'Everything was made in him, and without him was made nothing of that which was made.' (Prologue of John's Gospel)...

God's complete generosity is revealed in the Incarnation — nothing is held back. The religious world that humans develop cannot contain this mystery: God does not come as an angel, or a burst of light, nor even as an Idea or a vision — ***God comes as a baby!***"

(William Short, OFM, *The Franciscans* [Phoenix, AZ,: Tau Publishers, 2012], 106-7).

## Our Relationship with the Rest of Creation: How can we save a planet in peril?[49]

As was noted in chapter 2, the Franciscan Intellectual Tradition emphasizes the connection between Jesus (God's Word-become-human) and creation (another physical expression of God's Word). It is to the insights that Franciscan Intellectual Tradition offers in healing our damaged relationship with creation that we now turn. With increasing unison, scientists are pointing to an ecological crisis that faces our world. Various interrelated ecological issues, including climate change, pollution, species extinction, deforestation, and ozone depletion, threaten our planet and our very own survival. Although scientists have explained the harm that we have done and continue to do to the planet as well as

---

[49] Creation is used to refer to all that God has created, especially our physical environment, without forgetting that we, too, are a part of creation. The term "creation" is normally used in this book rather than "nature" or "environment" in order to remind us of our world's sacred connection to its Creator.

the probable consequences of continuing on our current course, humans have not significantly altered their behavior in ways that would prevent further damage to the environment and what some predict could be an ecological catastrophe. What might it take to convince us to demonstrate more care for the world around us and prevent irreparable damage to the environment? What insights does the Franciscan Intellectual Tradition offer as we face this crisis?

### THE EXAMPLE OF FRANCIS

Francis' own approach to and understanding of physical creation has much to teach us. On a most basic level (and as will be explained in greater detail below), Francis saw the physical world as good. That the physical world is good might seem obvious to some, but it certainly has not been a universally held belief—neither during the time of Francis nor today.[50] During Francis own day, a group called the Cathars argued that the physical world was evil (or at least irrelevant) and emphasized humanity's spiritual (vs. its physical) nature. Even today, there are a number of people of religious faith who view physical creation as something that threatens our spiritual well-being. Some others of religious conviction would argue that what happens to the physical world is largely irrelevant because all that ultimately matters is our spiritual well-being and spending eternity with God. Again, Francis saw the *goodness* of physical creation.

Francis' approach to and understanding of creation is probably best and most explicitly demonstrated through the *Canticle of the Creatures*, a prayer set to song that he wrote nearly a year before the end of his life at a time when he was likely almost entirely blind. There are three basic elements of his understanding of creation that are revealed in this Canticle:

1) a belief that God is to be encountered through the beauty of creation,
2) a sense of interconnectedness with the rest of creation, and
3) an awareness of creation's inherent worth apart from its usefulness to humans.

---

[50] The bible, too, points to the goodness of all creation. For example, in the first story of creation (Genesis 1-2:4a), which was probably written nearly 2,500 years ago, God declares creation to be good. This creation story, however, stood in stark contrast to other creation myths in different middle-eastern cultures which described creation as the accidental result of warring and sometimes evil gods.

First and perhaps most importantly, the Canticle demonstrates how Francis saw the world through eyes that allowed him to see the real depth, beauty and goodness of creation, all of which was a reflection of God's own beauty, goodness, and love. In this sense, the Canticle points to how Francis encountered God through the splendor of creation. For example, Francis points to his encounter with God through creation when he states that Brother Sun bears a resemblance to God. Francis teaches us that, just as we can learn something about an artist through a work of art that she has created, so we can learn something about God from God's work of art: all of creation. We call this worldview that holds that God can be encountered through physical creation a *sacramental* worldview. Again, a sacrament, in its most general sense, is something through which God is revealed to us and through which we can encounter God. For Francis, all of creation was a sacrament. Creation was a means through which he could encounter the love of the Creator.

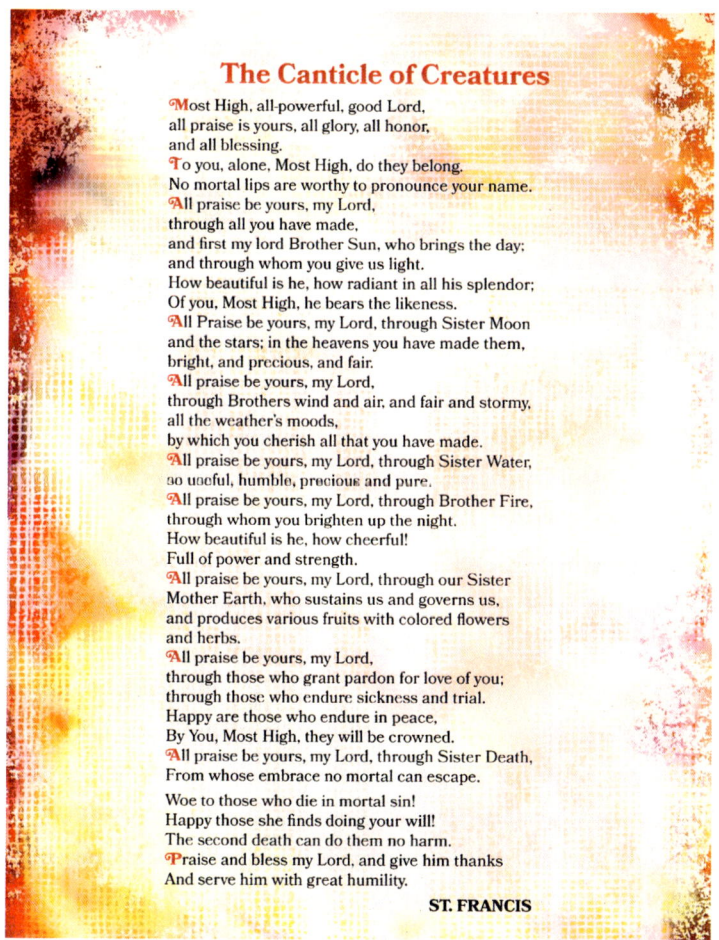

**The Canticle of Creatures**

Most High, all-powerful, good Lord,
all praise is yours, all glory, all honor,
and all blessing.
To you, alone, Most High, do they belong.
No mortal lips are worthy to pronounce your name.
All praise be yours, my Lord,
through all you have made,
and first my lord Brother Sun, who brings the day;
and through whom you give us light.
How beautiful is he, how radiant in all his splendor;
Of you, Most High, he bears the likeness.
All Praise be yours, my Lord, through Sister Moon
and the stars; in the heavens you have made them,
bright, and precious, and fair.
All praise be yours, my Lord,
through Brothers wind and air, and fair and stormy,
all the weather's moods,
by which you cherish all that you have made.
All praise be yours, my Lord, through Sister Water,
so useful, humble, precious and pure.
All praise be yours, my Lord, through Brother Fire,
through whom you brighten up the night.
How beautiful is he, how cheerful!
Full of power and strength.
All praise be yours, my Lord, through our Sister
Mother Earth, who sustains us and governs us,
and produces various fruits with colored flowers
and herbs.
All praise be yours, my Lord,
through those who grant pardon for love of you;
through those who endure sickness and trial.
Happy are those who endure in peace,
By You, Most High, they will be crowned.
All praise be yours, my Lord, through Sister Death,
From whose embrace no mortal can escape.
Woe to those who die in mortal sin!
Happy those she finds doing your will!
The second death can do them no harm.
Praise and bless my Lord, and give him thanks
And serve him with great humility.

**ST. FRANCIS**

In addition to demonstrating Francis' sacramental worldview, the Canticle also reveals to us the degree to which he saw his interrelatedness with all of creation.[51] He did not see himself as set apart from or above the rest of creation. Significantly, Francis saw himself as a part of creation and as a creature among other creatures created by the same all good and loving God. This sense of mutuality is reflected in the fact that Francis addresses the different elements of creation as brother, sister, and mother. He was at peace in and with creation because he took the time to enter into relationship with physical creation. Francis detached himself from his concerns, walked in the beauty of creation, and genuinely appreciated all that he saw.

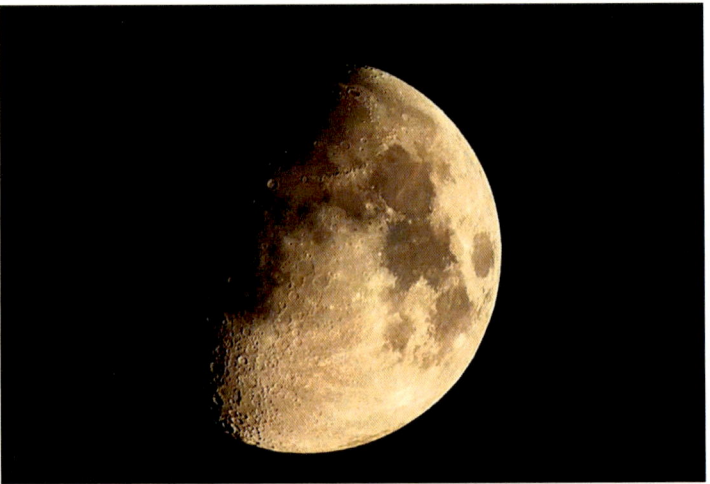

The Canticle not only reflects the sense of interrelationship that Francis had with all of creation, it also reveals his belief that *all* of creation has inherent worth and value apart from its usefulness to humans. This belief is reflected in Francis' observations that all creation, and not just humanity, gives praise to God. For example, in the Canticle Francis prays, "Praised be you, Lord, *through* Sister Moon" and "*through* Brother Wind." Francis held that elements of creation gave praise to God just by being what God created them to be. In this sense, a stone gives praise to the Creator by its very existence as a stone and an ant gives praise to God just by being what it was created to be: an ant! For Francis, elements of

---

[51] Francis was far ahead of his time in his understanding of and appreciation for our interconnectedness with the rest of creation. He saw himself as part of what today we might call the web of life. Science today teaches us how all of elements of the physical environment are intricately connected and interdependent in a delicately balanced circle of life.

creation have dignity, value, and worth in and of themselves, not just because of some use they serve for humans.

There is much to learn from Francis' understanding of creation. Our treatment of creation quite possibly would be positively impacted if we, like Francis, were to view creation as sacred, understand our interrelationship with all creation, and acknowledge the inherent value and worth of every creature.

### LAUDATO SI'

> St. Francis' attitudes towards creation are echoed in Pope Francis' encyclical (official teaching letter) *Laudato Si': On Care for Our Common Home*. [The name of this encyclical itself is taken from St. Francis' *Canticle of the Creatures*, in which St. Francis states "Praised be you, my Lord...." "Laudato Si'" is Italian for "Praised be."] Pope Francis points to the manner in which God is encountered through creation [par. 9 and 85], urges us to see our interrelatedness with all of creation [par. 137], and asserts that creation has inherent value apart from its usefulness to human beings [par. 84.]. Extremely significantly, Pope Francis argues that there is a close relationship between care for creation, care for the poor and vulnerable of the world, and issues of peace and justice, a relationship that St. Francis himself modeled and recognized [par. 10]. St. Francis might also be seen as a model of the kind of conversion away from consumerism that Pope Francis says will be necessary for us to avoid ecological catastrophe [par. 222]. In short, St. Francis moved from finding a meaning and fulfillment in the consumption of things to finding meaning and fulfillment in his relationships with God and others. Both St. Francis and Pope Francis teach us that we do not have to give in to the demands of our consumer-driven society and suffer from the havoc such consumerism wreaks on the well-being of our planet.

### *BONAVENTURE AND SCOTUS: GIVING THEOLOGICAL EXPRESSION TO THE EXAMPLE OF FRANCIS*

The great Franciscan thinkers of the 13th Century further underlined an obligation to recognize the sacredness of creation as they developed and expressed Francis' own insights into seeing the Creator reflected through creation. As noted in chapter 2, according to Bonaventure, by "reading the Book of Creation," i.e., by reflecting on the wonder of the world around us and truly seeing the physical world for what it is, we can come to know the author of the book: God. Our obligation to care for and not abuse creation is therefore affirmed because it is a means by which God is revealed to us.

Bonaventure's emphasis on the connection between the Incarnation and creation also underlines the great value of creation as well as our consequent need to respect and care for it. While Jesus is the ultimate way that God has chosen to share himself with us and has revealed himself to us, the Gospel of John (1:3) teaches us that *all* of creation came into being through God's Word, who became human in the person of Jesus. Therefore, there is a close and important relationship between Jesus and creation. According to the Franciscan Tradition, because there is this direct relationship between Jesus, our relationship with creation can help us to know Jesus and our relationship with Jesus can deepen our appreciation for goodness and wonder of creation. Furthermore, because all of creation came into being through God's Word, all of creation is a manifestation or sacrament (again, something physical through which God is revealed) of God. So, as was noted in chapter 2, while Jesus is the ultimate Incarnation of God (the ultimate way God has been physically or bodily revealed in the world), in a sense every creature becomes a "little incarnation" of God's presence (or a way that the Word or Son of God has been given "flesh" in the world). A Franciscan appreciation for the way every creature is a physical expression of God heightens our sense of the sacredness of creation and reminds us that by caring for and respecting creation we can also show respect and reverence for the Creator.

A deeper understanding of Bonaventure's system of creation coming from, revealing, and returning to God (chapter 2) could also lead us to a deeper appreciation of the dignity and sacredness of creation and to greater care for it. Creation clearly has inherent value, worth, and sacredness given that creation came forth from God and continues to reveal God. Bonaventure's emphasis that all creation is being renewed by Christ and being brought back to God further underlines the fact that creation has value to God as it should have for us.

Like Bonaventure, Scotus explains to us the depths of the sacredness of creation and provides us with a firm theological foundation for a need to care for creation. First, creation should be respected as an expression of God's love. As noted earlier, Scotus emphasized that God is completely free and is not forced by circumstances into anything. Rather, according to Scotus, God created because God wished to share God's self and love with something. Furthermore, creation has inherent value because this world served as the most perfect backdrop for the ultimate expression of God's love: God becoming human in the person of Jesus in the Incarnation.[52] Most profoundly, Scotus' teaching about the *haecceitas* of every creature, that unique quality that makes every creature what it is,[53] underscores the inherent worth and dignity of all of creatures that results from the fact that they were lovingly and individually willed into existence by God.

Both Francis and the important Franciscan thinkers after him have emphasized the connection between the Creator and creation. The Franciscan Intellectual Tradition teaches us to see creation as sacred because we can come to know the Creator through creation, which came into being through the very Word of God that became human in the person of Jesus, and to see our relatedness to all of creation. The Franciscan Intellectual Tradition also emphasizes that creation has value and worth in and of itself and beyond any service or use it may have for humans. The Tradition teaches us to see the world through different lenses, lenses that see the wonder, beauty and sacredness of creation. In doing so we will see the world on a deeper level for what it really is: the revelation and dwelling place of God where we can encounter God if only our eyes are opened to God's presence in the world. While scientists have explained how our attitudes and behaviors have and are negatively impacting creation and the inevitable consequences of what will happen to our planet if we do not change our ways, we still seem intent on not changing our ways. Perhaps the insights of the Franciscan Intellectual Tradition and the worldview it provides are just what is needed to change not only the way we view the world but also our attitudes and behaviors so that we can heal our relationship with creation and ensure the health of the planet for current and future generations.[54]

**Franciscan focus: We can begin to heal our relationship with creation by recognizing its sacredness, seeing our interrelatedness with it, and recognizing its own inherent worth.**

---

[52] As noted in chapter 2, within the Franciscan Tradition, creation is seen as the perfect backdrop for the Incarnation because creation came into being through the Son (or "Word"), who became human in the person of Jesus.

[53] See chapter 2. The implications of *haecceitas* will expanded upon in the section below on human dignity.

[54] Catholic Social Teaching emphasizes that care for the environment is also care for the poor and disadvantaged, who are often most immediately and directly impacted by damage done to the environment.

## MORALITY: IS IT REALLY ALL ABOUT RULES AND GUILT?

Many people in today's culture automatically tune out when the term "morality" is brought up. Often this is because morality is associated primarily with a list of prohibitive laws coming down from some institutional authority "out there." But what if our understanding of morality could be refocused to see that morality is really something positive because it seeks to explain how one might live human life to its fullest? The Franciscan Intellectual Tradition takes just such a positive approach to morality.

In the previous section we saw how Francis believed that God could be encountered through the beauty of creation. There is a balance and harmony in creation that we instinctively find beautiful. The Franciscan Intellectual Tradition teaches that our encounter with the beauty of God as revealed through the world can lead us to transform our lives to reflect that beauty of God in our behavior and attitudes. Francis' own encounter with God through creation led him to a process of conversion by which he gradually attuned his own life to better reflect God's own love by becoming more and more like Jesus. John Duns Scotus suggested that we can become artists who create beauty though the way that we live our lives. In this way, we cooperate with God, the Master Artist, in creating beauty in the world.

How do we lead lives that create beauty? We do so by becoming more God-like. As we have noted, the Franciscan Intellectual Tradition emphasizes God as an over-flowing relationship of love and goodness. God is self-giving love. The ultimate way that God revealed his love was through becoming human in the Incarnation. Jesus, the ultimate example of what it means to be human, demonstrated the ultimate meaning of self-giving love through his own free giving of himself on the cross. We are most fully human when we freely and generously give of ourselves as God did and does. In doing so, we think not only of ourselves but see our connectedness to others and give of ourselves for the good of others. This is a love that goes beyond a mere sense of human justice but reflects the merciful generosity of God. When we live lives of generous self-giving, we not only become more fully human but we become more like God to the point that we are brought more and more into closer union with God.

The Franciscan Intellectual Tradition does not see morality primarily in terms of do's and don'ts.[xii] Rather the Tradition emphasizes that we are to respond to the love God has shown us by reflecting that love in the world through love of our neighbor.

When we do, we become artists of beauty that are brought into closer union with God, the Master Artist. Morality does not have to be seen as an inhibiting list of negatives. In the Franciscan Tradition, morality is seen as a call to live fully human lives that reflect God's own beauty by embodying goodness and love through choices made. This move away from a focus on individual rules and laws and towards an emphasis on becoming agents of beauty through our choices and actions should not be seen as a moral "cop out." Rather, it is an immense challenge that calls us daily to become more God-like by laying down our lives for others in generous self-giving love as Jesus did[55]. Rather than being a "short cut" to escape moral responsibility, this understanding of morality calls us to a lifetime of conversion.

**Franciscan focus: Morality is a matter of drawing into closer relationship with God by responding to and reflecting God's own love in the world.**

### BEING CREATORS OF BEAUTY

"Moral living is better understood as a lifelong journey of ongoing conversion toward beauty: a way of seeing and living in the world. This journey is centered on the human capacity to respond freely and generously to the good. Within this vision, the moral person appears as an artisan whose vocation is to be creative of beauty in the world" (Mary Beth Ingham, "Moral Goodness and Beauty," in *The Franciscan Moral Vision: Responding to God's Love*, ed. Thomas A Nairn [St. Bonaventure, NY: Franciscan Institute Publications, 2013], 100).

---

[55] St. Francis prayed that he might reflect God's own self-giving love:

Your will be done on earth as in heaven: that we may always love you with our whole heart by always thinking of you, with our whole soul by always desiring you, whole mind by always directing all our intentions to you, and by seeking your glory in everything, with all our whole strength by exerting all our energies and affections of body and soul in the service of your love and nothing else; and we may love our neighbor as ourselves drawing them all to your love with our whole strength, by rejoicing in the good of others as in our own, by suffering with others at their misfortunes, and by giving offense to no one. *(Francis of Assisi, A Prayer Inspired by the Our Father, FA:ED I, line 5, 158-159).*

## ATTITUDE TOWARDS OWNERSHIP AND POSSESSION: DOES WHAT I CLAIM AS MY OWN DEFINE ME?

While "poverty" is an important concept in the lives of Francis and Clare and within the Franciscan Intellectual Tradition, it may also be a term that we do not see as applicable to our own lives. In this section we will examine what relevancy a Franciscan understanding of poverty as regards both material goods and attitudes (e.g., stubbornly holding onto one's own image, positions, interests, opinions, and worldview) might have for us today. As we will see, Franciscan poverty, in every sense, sheds light on the choice to turn either inwards towards ourselves or outwards towards life-giving and loving relationships with God, others, and creation.

As has been discussed in chapter 1, Francis experienced a deep conversion in his life that involved turning from finding meaning and fulfillment in material things to finding meaning and fulfillment in his relationships with God and others. He went from living a comfortable life as a member of the rising merchant class to rejecting ownership of any kind. In an even more radical abandonment, Clare rejected a privileged life among the nobility to embrace a life of absolute poverty and complete dependence on God in the Monastery of San Damiano. By rejecting ownership of things, Francis and Clare sought to acknowledge that ultimately everything is a gift from God and ultimately belongs to God. Furthermore, just as God clung to nothing for himself and was ultimately totally self-giving, so too Francis and Clare wanted to cling to nothing and to be completely open to sharing all that they had with others. In doing so, Francis and Clare affirmed the dignity of each human person by breaking out of social structures that emphasized that personal value was determined by how much one owned. Francis and Clare's rejection of material ownership was a way to reach out to and embrace those who otherwise were excluded from society. In short, Francis and Clare sought to remove the obstacle to their relationships with God and others that clinging to possessions could create.

As noted earlier, The Franciscan Intellectual Tradition stresses that our moral response to God's love is best lived out through lives of generous self-giving, not through an unhealthy "clinging" to what is ours, whether this be material possessions or our self-projected image, positions, time, and interests.[56]

---

[56] Francis develops an understanding of poverty that goes beyond material poverty in his *Admonitions* to his followers. For example, in Admonition XI he states, "That servant of God who does not become angry or disturbed at anyone lives correctly without

Our lives are to reflect God's beauty by mirroring God's own generous, self-giving love that is manifest not only through the gift of creation but especially through the Incarnation and in an ultimate way at the crucifixion.[57] Not only are we called not to selfishly cling to material possessions and our personal positions and interests, we are called to be generous with our time and talents when others are in need. In short, we are to "make room for love" in our lives. The Franciscan Intellectual Tradition further teaches that we should only be attached to things (whether items or attitudes) to the degree that they lead us to the Greatest Good: God. We are challenged to find meaning and ultimate satisfaction in our lives through those things that really matter: our self-giving and loving relationships with God and others.

**Franciscan Focus: An attitude of non-possessiveness helps us to make room in our lives for love and improved relationships.**

### Freedom from Self-centeredness

> "Agitation and anger, in fact, are for him the unmistakable sign of a possessive attitude—an attitude that is, moreover, most often unconscious. Francis rightly saw that at the base of the rupture between persons there is always a shrinking back on oneself, a secret desire for appropriation that makes man see everything in terms of himself: his personality, his idea, his project, his interests" (Leclerc, *The Song of the Dawn*, 45-6).

---

anything of his own" (FA:ED I, line 3, 133). Here the Latin phrase "*sine proprio*" translates as "without anything of his own" and clearly indicates that Francis' followers were to practice poverty of spirit as well as physical poverty.

[57] In the Bible, Paul describes Jesus' self-emptying in this manner:

"Who, being in very nature God, did not consider equality with God something to be used to his own advantage; rather, he made himself nothing by taking the very nature of a servant, being made in human likeness. And being found in appearance as a man, he humbled himself by becoming obedient to death— even death on a cross!

Therefore God exalted him to the highest place and gave him the name that is above every name, that at the name of Jesus every knee should bow, in heaven and on earth and under the earth, and every tongue acknowledge that Jesus Christ is Lord, to the glory of God the Father" (Phil. 2:6-11).

## THE VALUE OF LIFE: DOES EVERY HUMAN LIFE *REALLY* MATTER?

The next area of the Franciscan Intellectual Tradition that has great relevancy for today's world is closely related to the Franciscan recognition of the value of all of creation. As has been seen, Francis respected the inherent value and dignity of every creature as an expression of God's love and beauty. This was true in a special way as regards human beings. Because the first creation story in the Book of Genesis teaches that humankind is created in the image and likeness of God (Gn. 1:27), Francis acknowledged the dignity of every human being as a reflection of God and recognized the spark of the divine in every person that he encountered.[58] In particular, as we have noted, Francis reached out to and embraced those who were considered to be the lowest members of society: the poor, the sick, and the vulnerable. It was through his embrace of the lepers that he had once found so repugnant that he encountered Christ. It was through this embrace that he found genuine meaning and purpose in life. Francis challenges us to think about who the marginalized and most vulnerable members of our society are and our own attitudes towards them. He encourages us to acknowledge the inherent dignity of those who are most in need by reaching out to support them.[xiii]

Scotus' concept of *haecceitas* is very much related to an affirmation of the inherent dignity of every creature, especially every human being. As we have seen, according to Scotus, every creature is *individually* loved into existence by God and has a special *"thisness"* that makes it unique and unlike any other creature. This is as true for human beings as it is for other creatures. The Franciscan Intellectual Tradition challenges us, therefore, to treat each and every person we encounter as having inestimable value and dignity because he or she possesses a *thisness* given that he or she has been lovingly, individually, deliberately, and uniquely willed into existence by God. Today we realize how often the dignity of human life is trivialized: from abortion to euthanasia, from war and torture to unjust treatment of immigrants, from poverty and unjust economic systems to famine and disease, from lack of respect for those we encounter in our daily lives to prejudices of all kinds. The Franciscan Intellectual Tradition encourages us not only to acknowledge the dignity of all human life but to do all that we can to promote respect for that dignity whenever we find it ignored or abused.

---

[58] Francis stood in awe of the state of "great excellence" in which God placed the human race but also called upon his followers to mindful of their own ability to turn from God and of the fact that all that anyone is is a gift from God. Thus, we should approach God and others from a position of humility (*The Admonitions*, FA:ED I, Admonition V, 131).

**Franciscan Focus: Every human being has an inestimable value because he or she has been individually willed and loved into existence by God and created in God's own image.**

## Approaching World Religions: Do religious differences have to lead to destructive divisions?

As noted in the brief introduction to the life of Francis in chapter 1, Francis' encounter with the Sultan had a profound impact on his life and reshaped how he viewed others of different religions. Francis did not fight with the Sultan. Rather, he saw the good that was in him and entered into a respectful dialogue with him. Both Francis and the Sultan remained firmly rooted within their own faith while remaining respectful of and open to the faith positions of the "religious other." There is even evidence that Francis was open to how the Sultan could provide insights into how to live his own Christian faith more deeply. For example, some argue that Francis' *Praises of God* was influenced by the Islamic titles for God that emphasize God's grandeur and indescribable nature.[59]

The Praises of God
(Edition of Duane Lapsanski and Kajetan Esser)[60]
You are the holy Lord God
Who does wonderful things. Ps 77:15 [Vulgate, Ps 76:15]
You are strong. You are great. Ps 86:10 [Vulgate, Ps 85:10]
You are the most high.
You are the almighty king. You holy Father, Jn 17:11
King of heaven and earth. Mt 11:25
You are three and one, the Lord God of gods; Ps 136:2 [Vulgate, Ps 135:2]
You are the good, all good, the highest good,
Lord God living and true. 1 Thes 1:9
You are love, charity; You are wisdom, You are humility,
You are patience, You are beauty, You are meekness, Ps 71:5 [Vulgate, Ps 70:5]
You are security, You are rest,
You are gladness and joy, You are our hope, You are justice,
You are moderation, You are all our riches to sufficiency.
You are beauty, You are meekness,
You are the protector, Ps 31:5 [Vulgate, Ps 30:5]
You are our custodian and defender,

---

[59] Jack Wintz, O.F.M., "Franciscans and Muslims: Eight Centuries of Seeking God," accessed at: https://www.franciscanmedia.org/franciscans-and-muslims-eight-centuries-of-seeking-god.

[60] *The Praises of God*, FA:ED 1,109.

> You are strength, Ps 43:2 [Vulgate, Ps 42:2]
> You are refreshment.
> You are our hope,
> You are our faith, You are our charity,
> You are all our sweetness, You are our eternal life:
> Great and wonderful Lord, Almighty God, Merciful Savior.

In short, through his encounter with the Sultan, Francis learned to see the good in those whose religious faith looked different than his own. [xiv] Furthermore, because Francis was able to see God revealed through all of the world, he was able to see God revealed through people who were of a different faith. The later Franciscan intellectual tradition also emphasized that belief that God was revealed through *all* of creation. For example, Bonaventure's understanding that creation reveals God implies that God can be encountered through "the other," one who might look, act, or believe differently than we do.

Our world might be a very different place if it were to adopt the Franciscan approach towards the "religious other." Sometimes, those of one religious group hold an exclusivist position towards God. They believe that only their particular understanding of God is valid and dismiss those who do not believe as they do. Tensions resulting from a lack of respect for those who believe differently have even scandalously led people to kill in the name of God. The Franciscan Intellectual Tradition views such religious narrow-mindedness and intolerance as completely contrary to the way the infinitely good and loving God is revealed in the world. This Tradition respects persons of all faiths and views each encounter with another as an opportunity to draw closer to the God who created us all. Following the model of Francis, the Franciscan Intellectual Tradition calls us to witness to our own faith through the example of our lives and a respectful and joyful sharing of the Gospel. Without compromising our own faith positions, we can still be open to the wisdom and insights gained from the religious perspectives of others. In fact, such a respect and openness can even help one to deepen one's own faith tradition and relationship with God. An approach based on respectful dialogue between peoples of different religious belief as demonstrated by Francis and the Sultan can be a pathway to peace and justice.

**Franciscan Focus: God can be encountered through respect for those of different religious beliefs.**

## A WORLD IN CONFLICT: DOES PEACE REALLY BEGIN WITH ME?

Francis was an agent of God's peace. The greeting Francis and his friars used as they went out to serve in the world was "Peace and all good!" One legendary story about Francis involves a wolf that was terrorizing the town of Gubbio in Italy. Anyone who dared to leave the protective walls of the city was likely to be killed by the wolf. Having decided to make peace between the wolf and the citizens of Gubbio, Francis went out to Francis helped the citizens of Gubbio and the wolf to understand their mutual fear and then helped them arrive at an agreement by which they could peaceably depend on each other. The story of the Wolf of Gubbio demonstrates how a humble awareness of one's relatedness to others can lead to reconciliation and peace.

Francis' *Canticle of the Creatures*, in which he describes the interrelatedness of all creation, has already been explained. As noted in chapter 1, Francis composed the first part of the Canticle about a year before he died, a time at which he was likely mostly blind, and eventually added two more stanzas to the Canticle before he died —one which dealt with peace and the other in which he called death a "sister." It is the stanza that deals with peace that is most relevant here. In this stanza, Francis prays:

> Praised be You, my Lord, through those who give pardon for Your love (Mt 6:12),
> and bear infirmity and tribulation.
> Blessed are those who endure in peace
> For by You, Most High, shall they be crowned.[61]

Francis added this stanza when there was a conflict between the mayor and bishop of Assisi. In this stanza, Francis draws upon Jesus' Sermon on the Mount in the Gospel of Matthew (Matthew 5-6). Most specifically, Francis draws from the Lord's Prayer ["And forgive us our debts as we have forgiven our debtors" (Mt. 6:12)] and seems to be influenced by the Beatitude in which Jesus states, "Blessed are the peacemakers, for they will be called children of God" (Mt. 5:9). In the Canticle, Francis talks about the joy and blessings experienced by those who reconcile for God's sake. Francis realized that bitterness and resentment[62] only consume those who hold onto them and prevent people from experiencing healing and wholeness in their lives. Francis helps us to see that hatred only takes up room in our hearts, room that was meant for love of God and neighbor.

The Franciscan Intellectual Tradition, rooted in the life and example of Francis, also points to our interrelatedness with others. The Tradition emphasizes that we are all brothers and sisters given that we are all children of the same God. Furthermore, as noted above, Bonaventure emphasized God as a loving relationship.[xv] We, who are created in the image and likeness of God, are called to live in relationship with our brothers and sisters. To do so, we must have a sense of "solidarity," that is, a sense of our connectedness with and responsibility to others. Of course, one's connectedness with and responsibility to others increase the closer he/she is in relationship with them. But one's solidarity does not end with one's friends and family, or even with those in one's same city, state, or country. Rather, one is in relationship with all of humankind and, as noted earlier, even with all of creation. In a culture that very much emphasizes individualism and "doing one's own thing," the Franciscan

---

[61] Francis of Assisi, *The Canticle of the Creatures*, FA:ED I, verses 10-11, 113-114.

[62] Francis recognized that it was often having one's sense of ownership (even of one's own pride) being violated that led to anger and resentment. In this sense, a Franciscan attitude of refusing to appropriate anything to oneself (including the sense of being right) plays an important role in peace and reconciliation (see Leclerc, *The Song of the Dawn*, 44-46).

Intellectual Tradition's call to see our relatedness with and responsibility to others could serve as the basis for greater peace in our world.

This Tradition stresses not only a sense of interconnectedness but also an awareness that *all* of creation is an instrument though which God can be revealed in the world. This means that even an encounter with one I perceive as my enemy can be an opportunity in which I encounter God. In the Franciscan Intellectual Tradition, to be a moral human being is to live in right relationship with God, others, ourselves, and the rest of creation. We live moral lives and become most fully human by modeling our lives' on that of Jesus, who called us to see our relatedness with others and even to love our enemies (Mt. 5:44).[xvi]

**Franciscan Insight: Seeing our connectedness with and responsibility to others can serve as a foundation for peace in the world.**

### SOLIDARITY

What are some examples of a sense of solidarity? Some people, out of a sense of their interconnectedness with and responsibility to others, will only drink fair trade coffee, that is, coffee that is certified to have been grown and harvested by people working in safe conditions and for a fair wage. Similarly, out of a sense of solidarity, some refuse to buy clothing made by exploited laborers who experience deplorable working conditions. Care for creation can also flow from a sense of solidarity with others, both those on the planet now and those who will inherit the earth from us.

### JOY AND GRATITUDE: HOW CAN ONE SEE THE GOOD IN A WORLD WITH SO MANY TROUBLES?

Another important implication of the Franciscan Intellectual Tradition regards the attitude with which one views life. The Franciscan Intellectual Tradition teaches us that we can and should live life joyfully and full of gratitude. Francis lived life joyfully regardless of the circumstances in which he found himself. He was able to do this because he knew that he was always in the embrace of a good and loving God. As has been stated, Francis' worldview enabled him to see evidence of this God all around him. Furthermore, Francis found genuine joy in following in the footsteps of Jesus, even when such a course of life was not easy. The joy that Francis experienced was intimately connected with his sense of gratitude. Francis maintained a consciousness that all that is is a gift from God. First and foremost, Francis was grateful for the gift of God sharing himself and his love by becoming one of us in the Incarnation. While acknowledging that ultimately all things belong to God the Creator, Francis was also deeply moved by the gift of creation that surrounded him and that revealed God's overflowing love and goodness. Francis' awareness of the many gifts that God had given him led Francis to deep expressions of thankfulness.

The developing Franciscan Intellectual Tradition gave further grounding for the reasonableness of having an attitude of joy and gratitude in a world that sometimes seems filled with negativity. Bonaventure and Scotus emphasized God's goodness, love, and freedom. Furthermore, the Tradition's explanation of the foundational reason why God became one of us – because of God's desire to share his love, not just human sinfulness -- is seen as an affirmation of the goodness of humanity. Scotus' concept of *haecceitas* also points to the uniqueness, goodness, and beauty of not only every person but of every creature. In short, while realistic about human sinfulness and suffering, the Franciscan Intellectual Tradition emphasizes God's generous love and the evidence of that love seen in the Incarnation, self-giving human relationships, and the beauty of all creation. There is much to be joyful about and thankful for.

It is not always easy to be joyful in a world that seems to be full of so much violence and suffering. We often think that joy must precede gratitude, but often it is the other way around. Francis' recognition of all that he could be grateful for led to deep sense of joy in his life. At times it might be challenging to be grateful for the entirety of our lives.[xvii] The Franciscan Intellectual Tradition teaches us to keep our eyes open for that for which we can be grateful, even in difficult circumstances. In fact, it is an attitude of gratefulness, even in such troubling circumstances, that leads to a worldview that enables one to find joy.

**Franciscan Focus: A grateful recognition of God's graciousness in our lives can lead to a sense of joy regardless of circumstances.**

## A constantly transforming world: How do I live in a world with so much change?

One sense of the word "contingency" refers to the quality of being possible but not necessary or certain. The concept of contingency relates to the lives of both Francis and Clare. As noted in chapter 1, neither Francis nor Clare believed themselves to be boxed in by the roles expected of them by their families and society. Francis' father expected Francis to follow in his footsteps as a cloth merchant. Francis was at least expected to conform to the norms of society by fitting into the emerging merchant class of his day with all of its aspirations for increased wealth, influence, and power. Francis rejected these expectations and followed a different path, the path along which he felt God calling him. Similarly, Clare did not feel confined by the expectations placed on her by family and society. Within her family, Clare was expected to fulfill the role of a noble lady either by marrying someone of another noble family in order to increase the power and social position of her own family or by entering a traditional community of nuns. Society, too, expected Clare to fulfill the role of nobility by seeing herself as separate from and above the rest of society. Clare rejected the expected role of a noble lady, much to the dismay of her family, by embracing the same life of radical poverty that Francis had embraced. In short, Francis and Clare did not accept the belief that things had to be the way they were just because that was the way that they were expected to be.

The Franciscan Intellectual Tradition further developed the notion of contingency as it was exemplified in the lives of Francis and Clare. As has been noted, Scotus believed that the only absolute necessity was God. All else was contingent, that is, did not have to be by necessity. Scotus held that God created out of God's love and goodness. God was not forced to create or do anything (including becoming human) because of circumstances. According to Scotus, God is absolute; all else is contingent and does not have to be the way it is.

The implications of this Franciscan concept of contingency are significant. First of all, this concept helps to free us from thinking that things have to be the way they are just because that is the way they always have been. The way things are in the world can change and we can work for that change. Related to this first point is the belief that we do not have to fit into the roles expected of us by society. Ultimately, the Franciscan concept of contingency energizes us to embrace, rather than to reject, the change we experience in a rapidly changing world. The Franciscan concept of contingency gives us firm grounding to be open to and embrace that change rather than resist it. It is in this world of change that we are to experience God and to share our experience of God. Thus, the Franciscan Intellectual Tradition can help us not only to survive but to flourish in an ever-changing world.

**Franciscan Focus: Things do not need to remain the way they have been. We can embrace a world of change confident that we are in the hands of a free and loving God.**

Perhaps you began this chapter skeptical that there were any ways that the Franciscan Intellectual Tradition might relate to our world. Hopefully, this chapter has demonstrated that the Franciscan Intellectual Tradition does provide many important insights as we seek to understand God, others, ourselves, our world, and the relationships between all of these. The Franciscan Intellectual Tradition is not wisdom that belongs only to a past era. It has great relevancy to all those who continue to ask the big questions of life and to a world that faces many challenges.

## QUESTIONS FOR REFLECTION AND DISCUSSION:

### JESUS:

1. The Franciscan approach to understanding God and Jesus was examined in the last chapter. How has the deeper exploration of the significance of the Franciscan Intellectual Tradition in this chapter further influenced your understanding of God and Jesus? Do you think that the Franciscan approach to understanding God and Jesus would resonate among those whom you know? Why/not?
2. This chapter mentioned that we are called to be an incarnational people, i.e., we are to put flesh on God's presence in the world. How does this thought strike you? Why? What might this look like in your own life?

### OUR RELATIONSHIP WITH THE REST OF CREATION:

3. How might the Franciscan Intellectual Tradition affect your own attitudes towards the environment? What impact do you think a Franciscan understanding of creation could have in the modern world? What could help you to see the world through different "lenses"?

*MORALITY*:

4. What do you find appealing about a Franciscan approach to morality? What do you find yourself resisting about this approach? What are the strengths and weakness of this approach?

*ATTITUDE TOWARDS OWNERSHIP AND POSSESSION*:

5. What insights might the Franciscan Intellectual Tradition offer our consumer-driven society?

*THE VALUE OF LIFE*:

6. What might lead our society to have more respect for the dignity of each individual life? Who are the outcasts that we are called to reach out to as Francis himself did?

*APPROACHING WORLD RELIGIONS*:

7. How has the Franciscan Intellectual Tradition affected your approach to different world religions?

*A WORLD IN CONFLICT*:

8. Within the Franciscan Intellectual Tradition, our relationships with God, others, creation, and ourselves are seen as interrelated. Do you agree? Why/not?
9. To what degree do you have a sense of solidarity with others? What kinds of things hinder our ability to see our interconnectedness with others?
10. How might the Franciscan Intellectual Tradition help promote a quest for peace in the world?

*JOY AND GRATITUDE*:

11. Does the Franciscan Intellectual Tradition provide adequate grounds for maintaining a joyful attitude? Why/not? How might a sense of gratitude affect one's worldview?

*A CONSTANTLY TRANSFORMING WORLD*:

12. What is your general attitude towards change in the world? What insights might the Franciscan Intellectual Tradition provide you for dealing with change?

**GENERAL:**

13. Are there other important insights that the Franciscan Intellectual Tradition might offer our world that were not brought up in this chapter?

# Conclusion

Why am I on this planet? How do I lead a meaningful and purposeful life?

We started out this book looking at some of the big questions of life. Francis and Clare wrestled with these same questions and came to certain conclusions in their own lives. As we have seen, great intellectual and spiritual figures like Bonaventure and Scotus continued to wrestle with these questions as they articulated and developed in a more academic and theological fashion the spiritual wisdom of Francis and Clare. We have explored how the Franciscan Intellectual Tradition that has developed can give us insights and new perspectives as we face the theological, spiritual, social, and personal challenges and questions of our world. This life-giving vision can change how we understand and view our lives. Yet the Franciscan Intellectual Tradition will have little impact if it remains words and nice thoughts on a page. You the reader can personally ask yourself how the Franciscan Intellectual Tradition might give you insights into your life and how you approach life's ultimate concerns. How might the Franciscan Intellectual Tradition help you to live a better and more fully human life? How might the Franciscan Intellectual Tradition influence the way you understand God, others, yourself, and the world and the relationships between all of these? The wisdom of the Franciscan Intellectual Tradition is gift waiting to be opened. It is up to us to receive, apply, and pass on this gift to a world in need.

## Questions for Reflection and Discussion:

1) What do you see as the greatest contribution of the Franciscan Intellectual Tradition?
2) What difference does the Franciscan worldview make? What impact could it possibly have?
3) What is the most significant way the Franciscan Intellectual Tradition might influence the way that you personally approach life?

# ENDNOTES

i. St. Augustine also wrote much about what Christians are to believe and how they are to act. Often his writings addressed controversies of the early Church. For example, in Augustine's age there was a dispute about whether God or we ourselves were primarily responsible for our own salvation (a period known as the Pelagian controversy). In this dispute, Augustine argued that our salvation was dependent ultimately upon God.

ii. Aristotle's four categories of classification constitute a critical element of his philosophical system. According to Aristotle, all beings (those that are physical and those which can be conceived of in the mind) fall into four categories. The first and most important category is substance: the core nature of a being which makes something what it is apart from its relationship to anything else. The other three categories (quantity, quality, and relationship) all have to do with how a being exists in reference to other beings. Aristotle also had a system of four types of "causes," or ways beings impact one another: efficient, material, formal, and final. Chief among these was his understanding of efficient cause, i.e., that which brings something else into effect or existence. Franciscan scholars judiciously and creatively used Aristotle's categories of classification and system of causes to describe theological realities (Osborne, *The Franciscan Intellectual Tradition*, 15-30).

iii. Plato saw reality as divided between the spiritual and the material, with the former being superior to the latter. For Plato, the goal of life was to liberate one's spiritual nature from one's physical nature (Ilia Delio, *Crucified Love: Bonaventure's Mysticism of the Crucified Christ* [Quincy, IL: Franciscan Press, 1999], 177).

iv. St. Bonaventure was born in Bagnoregio in modern-day Italy around 1217. He himself recounts how, during a serious illness as a child, he was saved through the intercession of Francis of Assisi. Around 1235, he enrolled as a student at the University of Paris. Influenced by Alexander of Hales, an important Theology faculty member who had become a Franciscan, Bonaventure himself became a Franciscan around 1243/4.

He eventually taught at Paris until 1257, when he was elected General Minister (or head) of the Franciscan Order. Although Bonaventure wrote works more academic in nature while at the University of Paris, as General Minister his works became more spiritual as he sought to address various issues arising in the Order. Important among these issues was the question as to whether the Order would live out Francis' vision radically or practically. In 1259, Bonaventure, feeling the pressures of his position, retreated to Mt. La Verna, the same mountain where Francis had received the stigmata in 1224. Here Bonaventure wrote one of the great classics of Christian spirituality: *The Journey of the Soul into God*. Bonaventure also wrote what became the definitive description of Francis' life, the *Major Legend* (1260-1263). Bonaventure remained General Minister until 1273, when he was named Cardinal Bishop of Albano. He died at the Council of Lyons in France in 1274. He was named a saint in 1482 and declared a doctor (important teacher) of the Church in 1588 (Paul Rout, *Francis and Bonaventure*, Great Christian Thinkers, Peter Vardy, ed. [Liguori, MO: Ligouri Publications, 1997], and J.M. Hammond, "St. Bonaventure," *New Catholic Encyclopedia*, 2nd ed., 2003).

v. John Duns Scotus was born in Scotland in 1265/6. His uncle Elias Duns was vicar general of the Scottish Franciscans, and John himself took vows in the Order around 1281. He completed 8 years of study of the Arts before going Oxford to study theology in 1290, the year in which he was ordained a priest. He completed 2 years of study of theology at Oxford before moving to the University of Paris in 1293 to attend lectures on Peter Lombard's *Sentence Commentaries*. Before formally completing the Mastership in theology at the Paris in 1305, he lectured at Cambridge, Oxford, and Paris. Around 1302 and again in 1307 John Duns Scotus was forced to leave Paris, where he was studying and teaching, amidst tensions between the pope and the French king. Scotus was particularly vulnerable to accusations of heresy during his second exile because of his theological arguments against a declaration of the Immaculate Conception of Mary. Scotus taught at the Franciscan House of Studies in Cologne, Germany, where he died on November 8, 1308, after just over a year of teaching. He is recognized as "blessed" by Franciscans. A formal process of canonization for John Duns Scotus was begun in 1905 (Eric Doyle, "Duns Scotus – A Man for All Time," in *My Heart's Quest: Collected Writings of Eric Doyle, Friar Minor, Theologian*, Josef Raischl, OFS, and André Cirino, OFM, eds. [Phoenix: Tau Publishing, 2013], 210-213).

vi. The Trinity is a relationship of persons, or ways of experiencing God. The persons of the Trinity (Father, Son, and Holy Spirit) are distinguishable only in relationship to each other. The Father is the unbegotten person of the Trinity, that is, the Father comes forth from no other source or being. The Son is the person of the Trinity eternally begotten (or generated) by the Father. "Eternally begotten" means that, while the Son comes forth from the Father, there never was a time that the Son did not exist. As begotten, the Son is of the same nature as the Father and images, or mirrors, the Father. As the Father is self-giving, so must the Son, as image of the Father, be self-giving. Therefore, the Son returns love to the Father. The Spirit, the third person of the Trinity, can be described as the dynamic, self-giving love shared between the Father and Son. God's love is freely poured out into the world and into us through the Spirit (Delio, *Simply Bonaventure,* 39-53).

vii. For example, because God is both simple and complex (God is one and is "simply" Being itself yet God is complex in that God goes far beyond any understanding we could have of God), so the created world is simple and yet very complex (Creation is made up of simple, basic elements and yet is incredibly complex in its diversity and pushes the limits of science to fully understand it) (Zachary Hayes "Christ, Word of God and Exemplar of Humanity: The Roots of Franciscan Christocentrism and Its Implications for Today," Custodians of the Tradition Series, CFIT and ESP-OFM, 2).

viii. Yet creation, too, exemplifies God in that it too is a physical manifestation of the Son (or Word), through whom it (creation) came into existence. Thus, one might refer to the Incarnation (capital I) of God in the person of Jesus Christ and to the incarnation (lower-case i) of God in all of creation. In short, in Bonaventure's theological concept of all creation reflecting or revealing God, there is a close connection between the Incarnation of God in the person of Jesus and the "incarnation" of God in all of creation. As noted in this chapter, the ultimate way God has ever been exemplified in the world is in the person of Jesus Christ. But God, according to Bonaventure, is also exemplified through all of creation, which was brought into existence through God's Son, the same Son that became flesh in the person of Jesus Christ. The very fact that God would become human and express himself through even the tiniest element of creation pointed to the humility of God, an attribute of God very much emphasized by Francis and the Franciscan Tradition.

ix. According to Bonaventure, humankind has a particular role to play in this return of all of creation into God. As the only creature to have free will, humankind is the only creature able to tarnish the special manner in which it reflects God. Humans do this through turning away from God's will through the abuse of free will. In Bonaventure's system, in order for creation to be returned to perfection in God, humankind must reflect God in the way it was originally meant to by conforming itself to the ultimate exemplarity (or revelation) of God: Jesus, who is God-become-human. In short, in order for the return of creation to God to be completed, humankind has to become like Jesus. In conforming itself to Jesus (God-become-human), humankind, which constitutes the highpoint of creation having been made in the image of God (Genesis 1:27), leads the rest of creation to Jesus Christ, who brings all things back to God. Thus, not only humankind is being brought to the perfection and union with God through Christ, but also all of creation.

x. Pope Francis, too, emphasizes a God of love and mercy. He calls us to be a joyful people focused on the love of God revealed to us through the person of Jesus. We are called to respond to that love by recognizing God present in our neighbors and by giving of ourselves for their good (Pope Francis, *The Joy of the Gospel: Evangelii Gaudium*, [Washington, DC: USCCB, 2013], par. 36 & 39, 19 & 20-21). Pope Francis frequently speaks of God's mercy: "…God never tires of forgiving us; we are the ones who tire of seeking his mercy. … No one can strip us of the dignity bestowed upon us by this boundless and unfailing love. With a tenderness which never disappoints, but is always capable of restoring our joy, he makes it possible for us to lift up our heads and to start anew" (*Evangelii Gaudium*, par. 3, 2).

xi. In this section we have seen how God's own humility as expressed in the Incarnation teaches us something about where God is to be found in our world today. According to the Gospel of Luke, because there was no room for Jesus' family in an inn, Jesus, God-become-human, had been born into the poor and humble conditions of a stable. According to this same Gospel, Jesus' birth was first announced to shepherds, dirty, rugged men who were far from the elites of society (Luke 5). Because of the Incarnation and God's great humility expressed through it, Francis believed that it was the poor and lowly—the least among us (Matthew 25)--that revealed the face of God. For Francis, one did not find God by trying to ascend to lofty heights of status, wealth, and power. To look there for God was to miss the entire point of the Incarnation. The

Franciscan Intellectual Tradition challenges us to consider: Who is the outcast of our own day? Who is pushed to the margins of our society? Who is unwanted, unseen, and unheard?

xii. Oftentimes freedom is viewed as the ability to do whatever one wants. The Franciscan Intellectual Tradition teaches that this understanding of freedom is skewed on a number of points. First of all, it denies our interrelationship with others and the way that our choices impact others. Furthermore, the FIT teaches that freedom is best defined by our ability to give ourselves to what is ultimately good and beautiful. In this sense, the more naturally making the choice to create beauty in a situation comes to a person, the freer that person truly is. Furthermore, following laws that guide us to making beautiful and self-giving choices also makes us freer.

xiii. In the Gospel of Luke (10:29-37), Jesus tells the parable of the Good Samaritan in which a Samaritan stops to help a man beaten and left for dead while a priest and a Levite ignore the man in need. How might we be like the Good Samaritan who recognized and affirmed the dignity of one in need?

xiv. In discussing those brothers who live among non-Christians, Francis asserts that they can testify to the Gospel not only in their words but also without words through the manner in which they live their lives (*The Earlier Rule*, FA:ED I, chap. XVI, lines 5-7, 74).

xv. Through its emphasis on the loving, communitarian nature of God, the Franciscan Intellectual Tradition points not only to the importance of our human relationships but also to the interdependency of all of our relationships. Our relationships with God are very much connected to, reflect, and influence our relationships with others, creation, and even ourselves. If one of these relationships is out of balance or wounded, all of the relationships are affected, just as an individual chime out of balance in a wind chime can disturb the balance and harmony of the entire wind chime (Mary Beth Ingham, *The Harmony of Goodness: Mutuality and Moral Living According to John Duns Scotus* [Quincy, IL: Franciscan Press, 1996]).

xvi. What does it mean to love our enemies? We are not asked to *like* everyone else. To *like* someone means to find that person agreeable. In reality, we don't always enjoy the company of every other person. We are called to *love* everyone else, including our enemies. To *love* others [as Francis did] means to respect them as children of God, to see the good that is in them, to want what is best for them, and to give them the same consideration that we would want given to ourselves. In interpreting the Our Father, Francis prays, "*Forgive us our trespasses ... As we forgive those who trespass against us:* And what we do not completely forgive, make us, Lord, forgive completely that we may truly love our enemies because of You and we may fervently intercede for them before You, *returning no evil for evil* and may we strive to help everyone in You" (*A Prayer Inspired by the Our Father*, FA:ED I, lines 7-8, 159). In *The Earlier Rule*, Francis, referring to Mt. 5:44, notes that one could even love one's enemies out of gratitude for the great spiritual aid that comes from loving them (FA:ED I, chap.XXII, lines 1-4, 79). See also C.S. Lewis, *Mere Christianity*, Book III, section 9.

xvii. Henri Nouwen proposes just such a challenge in his book *Can You Drink the Cup?* (revised edition [Notre Dame, IN: Ave Maria Press, 2006], 80).

# Selected Bibliography

Bonaventure. *The Works of Bonaventure: Cardinal, Seraphic Doctor, and Saint*. Translated by José de Vinck. 4 volumes. Paterson, NJ: St. Anthony Guild Press, 1970.

———. *The Soul's Journey into God, The Tree of Life, The Life of St. Francis*. Edited by Ewert Cousins. History of Christian Spirituality Series. Mahwah, NJ: Paulist Press, 1978.

*Clare of Assisi: Early Documents*. Edited by Regis Armstrong. New York: New City Press, 2006.

Cunningham, Lawrence S. *Francis of Assisi: Performing the Gospel Life*. Grand Rapids, MI: Eerdmans, 2004.

Delio, Ilia. *Crucified Love: Bonaventure's Mysticism of the Crucified Christ*. Quincy, IL: Franciscan Press, 1999.

———. *Simply Bonaventure: An Introduction to His Life, Thought, and Writings*. 2nd ed. New York: New City Press, 2013.

Delio, Ilia, Keith Douglas Warner, and Pamela Wood. *Care for Creation: A Franciscan Spirituality of the Earth*. Cincinnati: St. Anthony Messenger Press, 2008.

Doyle, Eric. "Duns Scotus – A Man for All Time." In *My Heart's Quest: Collected Writings of Eric Doyle, Friar Minor, Theologian*. Edited by Josef Raischl and André Cirino. Phoenix, AZ: Tau Publishing, 2013.

Francis. Apostolic Exhortation *The Joy of the Gospel: Evangelii Gaudium*. Washington, DC: USCCB, 2013.

———. *Encyclical Letter Laudato Si': On Care for Our Common Home*. Washington, DC: USCCB, 2015.

*Francis of Assisi: Early Documents*. Edited by Regis Armstrong, J.A. Wayne Hellmann, and William Short. 3 volumes. New York: New City Press, 1999-2001.

Galli, Mark. *Francis of Assisi and His World*. Downers Grove, IL: InterVarsity Press, 2002.

Hayes, Zachary. "Christ, Word of God and Exemplar of Humanity: The Roots of Franciscan Christocentrism and Its Implications for Today." *Custodians of the Tradition Series*. CFIT and ESP-OFM.

Horan, Daniel P. *Dating God: Live and Love in the Way of St. Francis*. Cincinnati: St. Anthony Messenger Press, 2012.

Ingham, Mary Beth. *The Harmony of Goodness: Mutuality and Moral Living According to John Duns Scotus.* Quincy, IL: Franciscan Press, 1996.

———. *Rejoicing in the Works of the Lord: Beauty in the Franciscan Tradition.* Franciscan Heritage Series, vol. 6. St. Bonaventure, NY: Franciscan Institute, 2013.

———. *Scotus for Dunces: An Introduction to the Subtle Doctor.* St. Bonaventure, NY: Franciscan Institute, 2012.

Leclerc, Eloi. *The Song of the Dawn.* Chicago: Franciscan Herald Press, 1977.

Nairn, Thomas A., ed. *The Franciscan Moral Vision: Responding to God's Love.* St. Bonaventure, NY: Franciscan Institute, 2013.

Osborne, Kenan B. *The Franciscan Intellectual Tradition: Tracing Its Origins and Identifying Its Central Components.* Franciscan Heritage Series, vol. 1. St. Bonaventure, NY: Franciscan Institute, 2003.

———. "The Franciscan Intellectual Tradition: What Is It? Why Is It Important?," *AFCU Journal 5*, no. 1 (2008): 1-25.

Rout, Paul. *Francis and Bonaventure. Great Christian Thinkers.* Series edited by Peter Vardy. Liguori, MO: Ligouri Publications, 1997.

Rausch, Thomas P. *Who Is Jesus?: An Introduction to Christology.* Collegeville, MN: Liturgical Press, 2003.

Short, William. *The Franciscans.* Phoenix, AZ: Tau Publishers, 2012.

Vauchez, André. *Francis of Assisi: The Life and Afterlife of a Medieval Saint.* Translated by Michael F. Cusato. New Haven, CT: Yale University Press, 2013.

Warren, Kathleen and Joy Hart. *In the Footprints of Francis and the Sultan: A Model for Peacemaking.* Cincinnati: Franciscan Media, 2013. DVD.

## Photo Credits

The following images have been granted permission by Painted Psalms Art Gallery, Oakville, MO.
>   Clothed in Splendor
>   Wolf of Gubbio
>   Path of Peace (the Sultan)
>   The Transitus
>   Canticle of the Sun
>   Cave of the Heart
>   The Creche of Greccio

The woodcut design is courtesy of Artestampa di Gastone Vignati
>   San Damiano

All other images are found in open sourced material